GREYSTONE'S
Creative Hands

EDITOR

Beverley Hilton

GREYSTONE PRESS/NEW YORK · TORONTO · LONDON

Volume 10

Contents

© Fratelli Fabri Editore, Milan 1966, 1967
Marshall Cavendish Limited 1970, 1971, 1972, 1973, 1975
Manufactured in the United States of America
Library of Congress Catalog Card No. 75-8338

Much of the material contained herein has
previously been published in separate parts
under the title Golden Hands.

Pattern Library

Bright wings
This needlepoint butter-fly pattern is taken from a rug measuring 3 feet by 5 feet. designed by Louis J. Gartner Jr. Originally inspired by a fabric design, the butterfly motifs are not confined by a border but have been allowed to run off the edge freely. The use of dark brown and white in the design contrasts in an exciting way with the bright colors, bringing them to life and achieving a feeling of movement. The original rug was worked in petit point on double mesh canvas, the threads split to make 20 stitches to the inch.

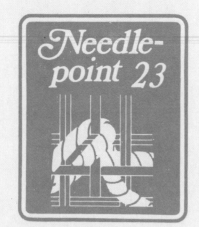

Hot city night

Once you have built up a repertoire of needlepoint stitches it is fascinating to combine them into a project. This panel incorporates many stitches which are built up into a cityscape of buildings seen by the light of the moon. Norwich stitch is used at the base of the fountain.

Special effects

Each stitch has been chosen for the special effect it creates. Particular examples are the leaf stitch effect on the trees in the square, the paving stones represented in cushion stitch and the blue blocks of satin stitch for a tiled roof. Under the arches the areas of shadow are created by using a mixture of pink and gray-pink yarns in the needle.

As well as an imaginative use of stitches, the colors and yarn textures contribute to the atmosphere of the picture. The town hall at the lower right-hand corner and nearly all the houses are in darkness, but a light shines from two windows, one in pink, the other giving a warm red glow. Other windows reflect the moonlight in plastic raffia, and in the square the spray of a fountain sparkles in silver beads. The soft warm tones of the colors are evocative of a hot summer night.

Materials you will need

☐ 20in by 22in single-weave white canvas with 14 threads to the inch (finished size $11\frac{1}{2}$in by $15\frac{3}{4}$in)
☐ Tapestry needle size 18
☐ Hardboard $11\frac{1}{2}$in by $15\frac{3}{4}$in
☐ Fine string
☐ Embroidery frame
☐ 5 skeins D.M.C. Matte Embroidery Cotton 2827; 7 skeins 2211
☐ 1 skein each D.M.C. 6-strand floss 211, 3041, 552
☐ 1 skein each D.M.C. Tapestry yarn 7535, 7157, 7996, 7259, 7492
☐ 2 skeins each 7318, 7602, 7157, 7292; 3 skeins 7247; 12 skeins 7241
☐ Small quantities purple wooden beads, small silver beads, dark blue plastic raffia

Working the panel

Work with the canvas in a frame, using the illustration as a chart. Begin by working the left-hand building first, then out and across the other buildings, filling in the background as you progress. If the background areas are left until the buildings are all completed, the worked stitches will have spread the threads of the canvas, thus pulling the remaining canvas threads too close together for easy stitching. Complete the panel by working the outer background on all four edges to the required depth.
Block the work (see Needlepoint chapter 5, page 112) and mount over the piece of hardboard (see Needlepoint chapter 19, page 752). The panel can be hung framed or unframed.

Stitch guide

1. Blocked satin stitch
2. Detached eyelets
3. Tent stitch
4. Rice stitch
5. Norwich stitch
6. French knots
7. Leaf stitch
8. Encroaching Gobelin stitch
9. Cushion stitch
10. Checker stitch
11. Parisian stitch
12. Tile stitch
13. Plaited stitch
14. Mosaic stitch
15. Satin stitch
16. Double cross-stitch
17. Raised chain band and darning worked on a foundation of encroaching Gobelin stitch

Norwich stitch worked over odd number of threads, in numbered sequence, in directions indicated

Raised chain band edged with darning stitch over a base of encroaching Gobelin stitch

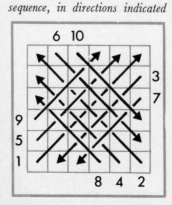

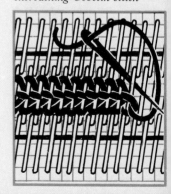

Filling squares for designs

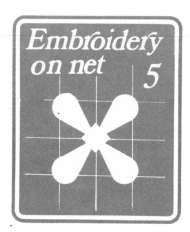

Embroidery on net 5

One of the most frequently used techniques in embroidery on net is to have a linen stitch filling with the shape of the motif strongly outlined. This is very simple to do and most effective. Once you have learned this technique, you can go on to building up pictures for which you can work out your own designs. This is based on counting squares and working the shape as neatly as possible into the squares, and finally defining the motif with the outline, as in the leaf motif. The screen illustrated shows a tree incorporating the leaf and a flower motif worked on a half-inch net specially made to fit the screen. For a finer effect, a ready-made quarter-inch mesh should be used. The result is distinctly oriental and very feminine for a bedroom.

Transferring a design onto net
Squared net has to be tackled like counted thread embroidery and the designs are transferred by counting the squares, usually from the center outward.

Tension
It is extremely important to keep the tension of the stitches even while working, but a frame can easily distort such an openwork fabric as net. The best solution is to baste small pieces of work onto a piece of stiff cardboard to support it while you work. With larger pieces it is best to hold the net in the hand and spread it out on a flat surface from time to time to check that it is not puckering.

Building up a design
When working a design, first fill in the squares to be included. For different effects, shapes can be outlined with running stitch, which is sometimes overcast for a stronger effect, or with darning stitch, which is sometimes worked in several thicknesses.

Linen stitch
This is a basic filling stitch which can be used either to fill in shapes or on its own to form the shapes. It consists of rows of alternated running stitch, worked first vertically and then horizontally and interwoven. Each square always contains an equal number of threads.
Fasten the thread to a knot in the net and working vertically, pass the thread alternately over and under the bars of the net. This can be worked in one square only or over several squares to fill a large area.
N.B. When laying the vertical threads remember that both the strands to the left and right of a vertical bar of net must run in and out in the same way, as the bar of net will form the alternating thread. In this way the pattern of the horizontal threads is not broken. Lay the horizontal threads by picking up alternate vertical threads. Work as many horizontal threads to each square as there are vertical ones to form an even filling.

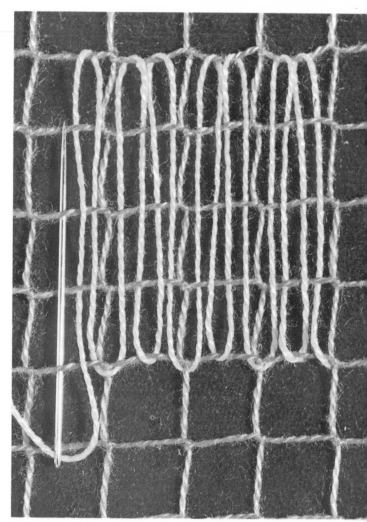

▲ *Laying the vertical threads which form the basis of linen stitch*
▼ *Working the interwoven horizontal threads for linen stitch*

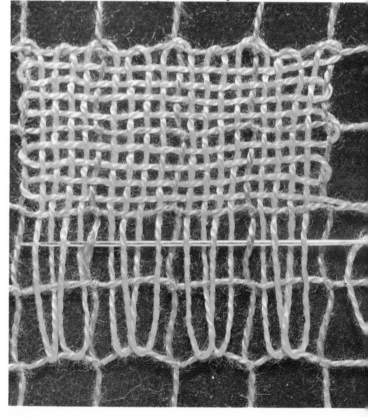

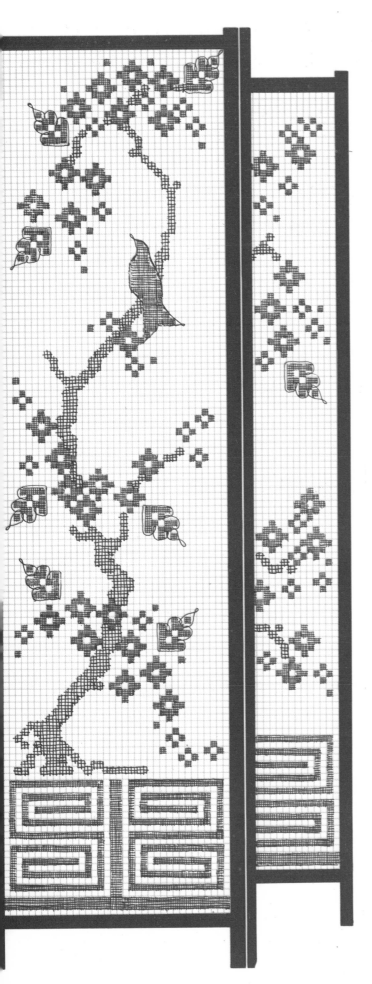

◄ *A pretty screen with an oriental tree design worked on half-inch net*

▲ *Outlined linen stitch leaf motif*
▼ *Four strand darning stitch outline*

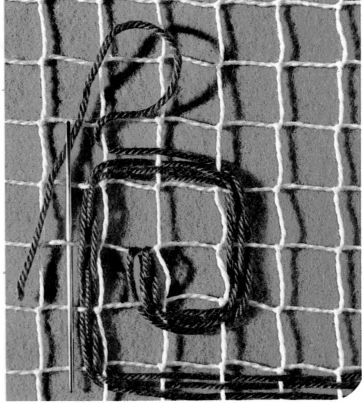

Matching tops for pants

Dress-making 50

Adapted from the Creative Hands basic dress pattern, these soft-line tops, with rouleau loop or tie fastening, are designed to be worn with the pants in Dressmaking chapters 48, page 956, and 49, page 974, making a stunning, complete pants outfit that is suitable for any occasion.

Suitable fabrics

Most soft blouse fabrics are suitable for these tops, as well as the more substantial fabrics like the knit and crêpe used here. If you buy a knit fabric for a garment fastened with rouleau loops, make sure that the knit is close and firm. Loops tend to stretch and gradually become too large for the buttons if they are made in a loose-knit jersey. Also the seams of the rouleau break and the loops become useless and untidy.

The patterns

A. The day tunic

The pattern pieces you will need are: Front, Back, sleeve, front facing and back neck facing, which should be made as follows:
Front and Back. Copy the Front and Back dress pattern pieces from the Creative Hands Pattern Pack given in Volume 22.
This is a slip-on garment which has no zipper opening. The Center Front seam is opened from the neckline down to a point of your own choosing, so mark the Center Front edge of the pattern where you want the opening to end, but make it long enough to get the garment over your head.
If you have made the basic dress and fitted it more than the original, and have altered the pattern accordingly, it is necessary to return the gentle curve of the orginal through the waistline in the side seams or the top will be too narrow to slip over your shoulders. Measure the length you want the tunic top to be and cut both Back and Front pattern pieces to that measurement. If you are going to wear the tunic belted, remember to make the pattern longer to allow for the fabric riding up under the belt.
Facings. To make the front facing pattern, lay the Front pattern piece along the edge of a sheet of paper and copy the Center Front from the opening mark to the neck edge and along the neckline and shoulder seam. Draw in the facing 2 inches wide at the shoulderline and 2 inches wide at the lower edge as shown (figure **1**). Also make a back neck facing (figure **2**).
Cut out the facing patterns, then pin the front facing to the Front of the new tunic pattern along the Center Front, with the edges meeting over a strip of paper so that the Front and front facing can be cut as one (figure **1**).
Sleeves. For the sleeve pattern, make the bishop sleeve version A (the full sleeve without cuff from Dressmaking chapter 44, page 874). If you are using a heavy fabric such as the double knit shown here, do not make the pattern quite as full.

*Evening overblouse, B, shown left
orn with flared pants in crepe*

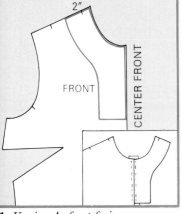

*Day tunic, A, shown right in jac-
uard jersey with cossacks in plain jersey*

2″

FRONT

CENTER FRONT

1. *Version A: front facing*
2. *Versions A and B: back neck facing*

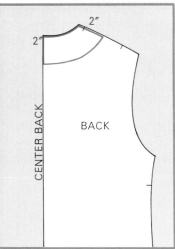

2″

2″

CENTER BACK

BACK

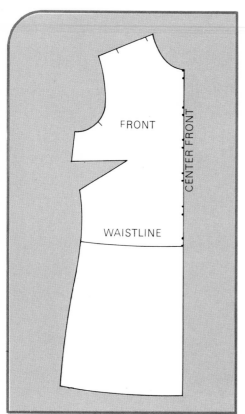

▲ 3. *Right Front version B: the loop positions*

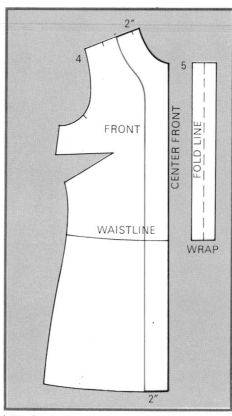

▲ *Version B:* **4.** *front facing:* **5.** *wrap pattern*

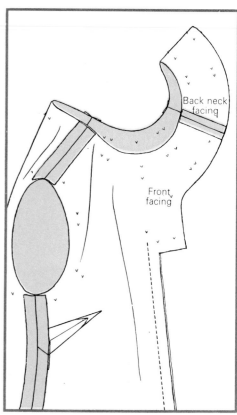

▲ **6.** *Version A: the stitched neck facings*

B. The evening overblouse

The pattern pieces you will need are: Front, Back, sleeve, cuff, front facing, back neck facing and wrap, which should be made as follows:

Front and Back. Copy the Front and Back dress pattern pieces from the Creative Hands Pattern Pack given in Vol. 22. This top has a front opening and can therefore be cut to the shape of a fitted pattern if you have altered the basic pattern accordingly.

The Center Front on the finished garment meets edge to edge and fastens down the front from neck to waist with rouleau loops and buttons.

To mark the Front pattern for buttoning, first take your front neck to waist measurement and mark this measurement on the Center Front of the pattern.

Then mark the positions for the loops which go on the right Front, $2\frac{1}{2}$ to 3 inches apart, between the neck and waistline (figure **3**).

Measure the length you want the overblouse to be and cut both Back and Front pattern pieces to that measurement.

Facings. To make the full length front facing pattern, lay the Front pattern piece on the edge of a sheet of paper, copy the neckline and the shoulder seam and make a facing as shown (figure **4**) which is 2 inches wide at both hem and shoulder edge. Also make a back neck facing as for the day version (see figure **2**).

998

Wrap. For the wrap on the left Front, cut a strip of paper 2 inches wide to the length of your front neck to waist measurement and mark the lengthwise center fold line (figure **5**).

If you prefer to leave the top two buttons undone, do not take the wrap to the neck edge, but from the waist to the last button that you are going to wear done up. This way the wrap will not show.

Sleeves and cuffs. For the sleeve and cuff pattern pieces, make the bishop sleeve or bishop sleeve version C (the full sleeve with fitted top and tapered cuff shown in Dressmaking chapter 44, page 874).

If you are using a heavier crêpe type fabric as shown in the picture, do not spread the pattern too full. Some of these fabrics are made only to resemble crêpe with the finishing treatment, while the basic weave—which in real crêpe consists of highly twisted crêpe yarns—is often plain and flat. The folding and draping qualities of the simulated crêpe fabric are therefore not the same as in real crêpe. If you cut the sleeves too full, the fullness will stand out not only around the wrist, where it looks beautiful, but also along the full length of the sleeve and will therefore look very bulky around the upper arm. So use the bishop sleeve version C, but cut the sleeve a little longer, especially at the curve in the wrist. This is a professional's trick used to give the impression of greater fullness.

Yardages and layouts

Make your own layout and calculate your yardage requirements as shown in Dressmaking chapter 46, page 916.

Start your yardage calculation for 36 inch wide fabric as follows: twice the length of the blouse, plus twice the length of the sleeve, plus $\frac{1}{2}$ yard for cutting a rouleau. Do not forget to add seam and hem allowances to the lengths.

Interfacing. The evening overblouse B, made in a fabric such as crêpe, will need the support of interfacing on the neck edge and the Center Front edge to the waistline.

You can use the back and front facing patterns for the interfacing. The cuffs also need interfacing, so make a small layout to work out the amount of interfacing you will need.

Making the tunics

A. The day tunic

This version can be made in two ways. You can stitch the side seams from underarm to hem or you can leave them open from the waist down in true cossack style. Pin, baste and fit the tunic. If you are going to wear it with a belt, try on the belt when deciding the length as soft fabric gathers up considerably when it is belted. Stitch the Center Front seam from the end of the opening to the hem, overcast, press.

▲ **7.** *Version A: the tied and knotted rouleau*

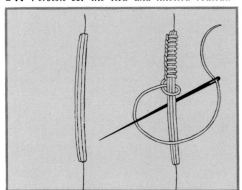

▲ **8.** *The bar carrier for a belted style*

Stitch the side bust darts and press.
Stitch the shoulder and side seams, finish seams and press. Make the hem.
If you have left the side seams open from the waist down, finish the hem at the seams as for the slit in the shorts (Dressmaking chapter 49, page 974, figure 4) and slip stitch the side seam allowances in place from waist to hem.

To finish the neck edge, stitch the back neck facing to the front facings at the shoulder seams (figure **6**). Trim the seams to $\frac{1}{2}$ inch and press open.
Pin and baste the joined facing to the inside of the neckline, raw edges even, with wrong sides facing and seamlines corresponding.
Trim the seam allowance on the neck edge to within a fraction of the seamline and finish the raw edge with a bias strip turned over the edge as for a rouleau type binding (see Dressmaking 25, p. 496).
Fasten the Center Front of the neck edge with a handmade loop and small button.
Cut a bias strip about 24 inches long to the width required for a $\frac{1}{4}$ inch wide rouleau.
Make a rouleau for the loops following all the steps given in Dressmaking 44, p. 874. Tuck in the ends of the finished, turned rouleau and handsew them together. Then tie a knot in the rouleau on each end. Finally, tie the rouleau into a bow and sew it to the neck edge to cover the button and loop fastening (figure **7**).

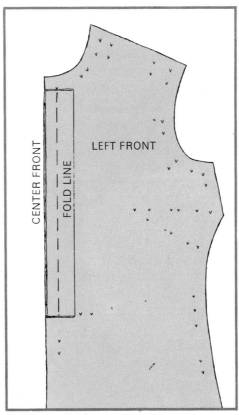

9. *Version B: the wrap basted in position*

Make the sleeves as shown in Dressmaking chapter 44, page 874, and stitch them in. If you want to wear a belt with the tunic, make a handworked carrier on each side seam at waist level (figure **8**).

B. Evening overblouse

Pin, baste and fit the overblouse. After fitting, rip the side and shoulder seams and work the Center Front first.
Make a rouleau for the loops following all the steps given in Dressmaking chapter 44 and prepare the loops for the chosen button size as shown in the same chapter. On the right Front, place a loop over each mark and hand sew to the seam allowance as for the loops on the tapered cuff. Fold the strip for the wrap lengthwise on the fold line, wrong sides facing, folding in the seam allowance at each end. Pin and baste the whole strip and press lightly. With raw edges even, pin and baste the wrap to the outside of the left Front along the Center Front seamline (figure **9**).
Stitch the side bust darts, and the body darts if you are using them. Press.
Stitch the side and shoulder seams, finish seams and press.
For interfacing the neck and front edges, lap the seam allowance of the back neck interfacing over the seam allowance of the front interfacing at the shoulder seams and stitch as shown in figure **4**, Dressmaking

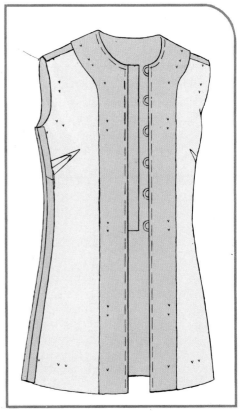

▲ **10.** *Version B: the stitched and turned facing*

chapter 37, page 734. Trim the seam allowances and pin and baste the interfacing to the inside of the overblouse.
Join the back neck and front facings at the shoulder seams. Trim the seam allowances to $\frac{1}{2}$ inch and press open.
With right sides facing, pin and baste the facing to the outside of the overblouse (the loops on the right side and the wrap on the left are hidden between overblouse and facing).
Stitch the facing in place along the Center Fronts and neck edge, trim and snip the seam allowances and turn the facing to the inside of the overblouse. Edge-baste and press (figure **10**).
Anchor the facing to the overblouse with small catch stitches at the waistline and around the back neck.
Make the hem.
Make the bishop sleeves as shown in Dressmaking chapter 44, page 874 and stitch them into the armholes of the overblouse.
Pin the edges of the Center Front so that they meet on the wrap, mark the positions for the buttons and sew on the buttons. At the waistline, stitch on a hook and bar to support the loop and button at the waist edge. Large buttons and loops are more decorative than functional, and if they are subjected to any strain it is best to support them with a small hook and bar. Or if, as with this overblouse, you have a wrap, you can use small snap fasteners instead of hooks.

Furnishing Fashion Flair

Cuddly cats and kittens

It can be really fun working a motif which is particularly cute and appealing, and these kittens are a good example. An obvious motif for a child's room, that can be appliquéd or embroidered, the kittens look especially charming with a real bell sewn to the collar.

1. *Twin kittens guard a comfortable pillow.*
2. *Decorate a little girl's clutch purse with an embroidered kitten.*
3. *The novelty of a window draft excluder appliquéd with a row of kittens would brighten any room.*
4. *Use the motif all around the hem of a child's bedspread.*

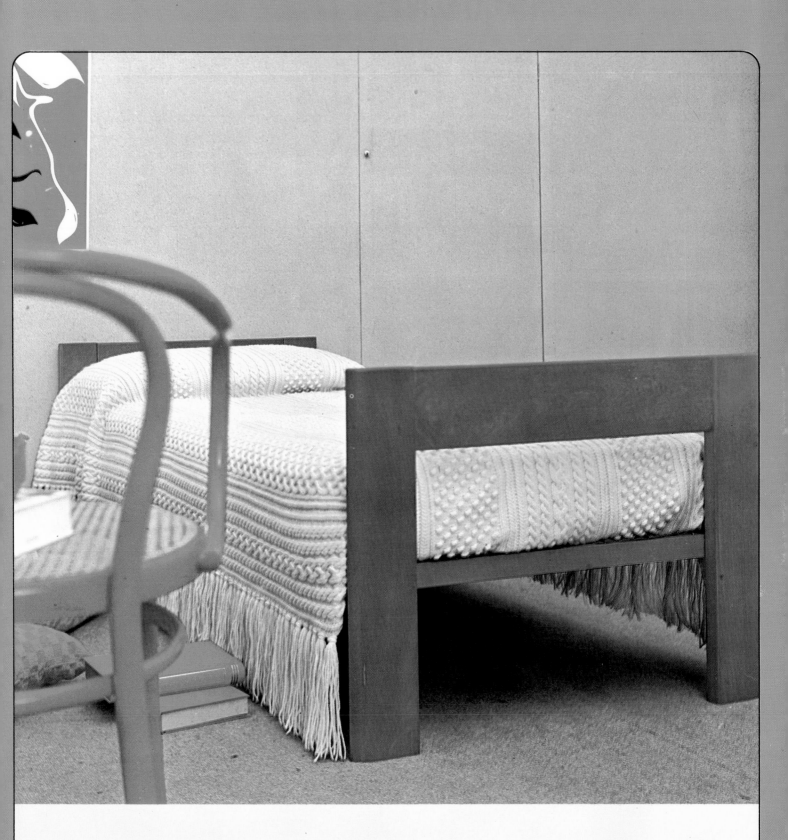

Pattern Library

Aran bedspread

Knitting Know-how 51, page 1002 deals with the derivation and formation of Aran patterns. This bedspread is a superb example of the effect-ive combination of cable stitches (see page 1002) and bobble and trellis stitches, which will be included in the next chapter. To make the bedspread, work out the width required for 7 separate panels and work out each section for the desired length. Use a natural fisherman yarn for a traditional effect and finish side edges with fringing.

Treasury of Aran stitches

▲ *Honeycomb stitch*

▲ *Lobster claw cable*

The Aran islands of Inishmore, Inishmaan and Inisheer, off the west coast of Ireland, are the home of the popular and richly textured knitting known as Aran. The Irish name for the thick, homespun wool used for Aran knitting is bainin, pronounced "bawneen," meaning natural, or white. It is also known as fisherman yarn. The traditional patterns show to their best advantage on this light-colored wool, although it is sometimes tinted with seaweed or moss dyes to produce pale, subtle shades. Practice the stitches in this chapter (use knitting worsted and No.5 (or Canadian No.8) needles if fisherman yarn is difficult to obtain) by knitting panels which can then be joined together to make unique-looking furnishings such as pillow covers, bedspreads, or afghans.

Like all folk crafts, the traditional Aran designs derive their inspiration from the daily life of the islanders. The rocks and cliff paths are called to mind by the stitches of zigzag patterns, while chunky bobbles and the fishermen's ropes are depicted by a vast number of cable variations which play a major part in most designs. The life under the sea which surrounds the islands is acknowledged in such designs as lobster claw cable. Religious symbolism appears in stitches such as Tree of Life, Trinity stitch and Ladder of Life, while everyday life is depicted in the ups and downs of marriage lines and in several different seed stitches (see single and double seed stitches in Knitting Know-how 5, p. 82). Even the industrious bee is remembered in honeycomb stitch.

Honeycomb stitch
Worked over a number of stitches divisible by 8.
1st row. *Sl 2 sts onto cable needle and hold at back of work, K2, K2 from cable needle—called C4B—sl 2 sts onto cable needle and hold at front of work, K2, K2 from cable needle—called C4F—rep from * to end.
2nd row. P to end.
3rd row. K to end.
4th row. P to end.
5th row. *C4F, C4B, rep from * to end.
6th row. P to end.
7th row. K to end.
8th row. P to end.
These 8 rows form the pattern and are repeated throughout. A variation of honeycomb stitch is made by working extra rows in stockinette stitch between the cable rows to elongate the design.

Ladder of Life
This is a simple design, depicting man's desire to do better and climb upward toward heaven. The rungs of the ladder are formed by purl rows worked on a stockinette stitch background.
Worked over a number of stitches divisible by 6, plus 1 (i.e. 37).
1st row. (RS) P1, *K5, P1, rep from * to end.

2nd row. K1, *P5, K1, rep from * to end.
3rd row. P to end.
4th row. K1, *P5, K1, rep from * to end.
These 4 rows form the pattern and are repeated throughout. The number of stitches between the vertical purl lines may be altered to suit the area to be covered, as may the number of rows worked between the ladder rungs.

Trinity stitch
This stitch derives its name from the method of working, which is "3 in one and 1 in 3." In England it goes by the name of blackberry stitch, while in Scotland it's called bramble stitch.
Worked over a number of stitches divisible by 4.
1st row. P to end.
2nd row. *K1, P1, K1 all into same st making 3 sts from one st, P3 tog to make one st from 3 sts, rep from * to end.
3rd row. P to end.
4th row. *P3 tog, K1, P1, K1 all into one st, rep from * to end.
These 4 rows form the pattern and are repeated throughout.

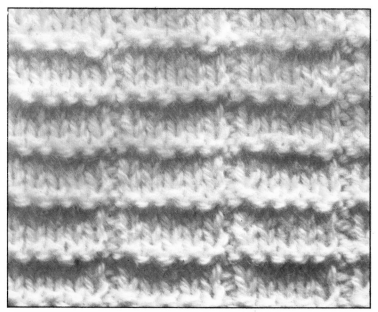

▲ *Ladder of Life*

▲ *Trinity stitch*

▲ *An unusual sampler of interlaced cables edged with a finishing panel of twisted stitches*

Lobster claw stitch

Worked over a number of stitches divisible by 9 (i.e. 45).

1st row. *P1, K7, P1, rep from * to end.

2nd row. *K1, P7, K1, rep from * to end.

3rd row. *P1, sl 2 sts onto cable needle and hold at back of work, K1, K2 from cable needle, K1, sl 1 st onto cable needle and hold at front of work, K2, K1 from cable needle, P1, rep from * to end.

4th row. *K1, P7, K1, rep from * to end.

These 4 rows form the pattern and are repeated throughout. The number of stitches over which the claw is worked and the number of rows between the cable rows may be altered, but too much alteration could change the appearance of the claw-like look.

Sample of interlaced cable stitches

This sample, worked over 64 sts, includes two types of cables which depict the fishermen's ropes, and is edged with a twisted stitch often used in Aran patterns.

1st row. (RS) K1, P1, K1y2rn, K2, P3, (K6, P3) twice, K12, (P3, K6) twice, P3, K1y2rn, K2, P1, K1.

2nd row. K2, P2, sl 1 keeping yarn on WS, K3, (P6, K3) twice, P12, K3, (P6, K3) twice, P2, sl 1 keeping yarn on WS, K2.

3rd row. K1, P1, sl long st onto cable needle and hold at front of work, K1y2rn, K1, K1 from cable needle—called CTw3—P3, (K6, P3) twice, K12, (P3, K6) twice, P3, CTw3, P1, K1.

4th row. As 2nd.

5th row. K1, P1, CTw3, P3, (sl next 3 sts onto cable needle and hold at front of work, K3, K3 from cable needle—called C6F—P3) twice, C6F twice, P3, (C6F, P3) twice, CTw3, P1, K1.

6th row. As 2nd.

7th row. As 1st, keeping CTw3 at each end.

8th row. As 2nd.

9th row. As 7th.

10th row. As 2nd.

11th row. K1, P1, CTw3, P3, (C6F, P3) twice, K3, sl next 3 sts onto cable needle and hold at back of work, K3, K3 from cable needle—called C6B—K3, P3, (C6F, P3) twice, CTw3, P1, K1.

12th row. As 2nd. *13th row*. As 7th.

Rows 2-13 form the pattern and are repeated throughout.

The puff-sleeved cardigan

This short-sleeved summer cardigan has been specially designed for a little girl to wear over a puff-sleeved dress to provide extra warmth without detracting from the design of the dress. Worked in one piece from the neck downward, the only seaming required is an underarm seam. Once knitting is completed, the garment is almost done because it requires so little finishing.

Sizes

Directions are for 22in chest. The figures in brackets [] refer to the 24 and 26in sizes

respectively. Length down center back, 9½[9¾:10¼]in. Sleeve seam, 2[2¼:2½]in.

Gauge
7 sts and 9½ rows to 1in over stockinette stitch worked on No.3 needles.

Materials
3-ply baby yarn
3[3:3] 1 oz skeins
One pair No.2 needles (or Canadian No. 11)
One pair No.3 needles (or Canadian No. 10)
Four small buttons

Cardigan

Beg at back neck.
Using No.3 needles, cast on 48[52:56] sts.
__1st row__ K.
__2nd row__ P.
__3rd row__ Inc in first st, K2, inc in next st, K10 for left sleeve, inc in next st, K2, inc in next st, K12[16:20] for back, inc in next st, K2, inc in next st, K10 for right sleeve, inc in next st, K2, inc in last st.
__4th row__ P.
__5th row__ K1, inc, K2, inc, K12, inc, K2, inc, K14[18:22], inc, K2, inc, K12, inc, K2, inc, K1.
__6th row__ P.
__7th row__ K2, inc, K2, inc, K14, inc, K2, inc, K16[20:24], inc, K2, inc, K14, inc, K2, inc, K2.
__8th row__ P.
Continue in this way inc 8 sts on every RS row until 10 rows of inc have been completed. 128[132:136] sts. P 1 row.

Shape sleeves
__23rd row__ K10, inc, K2, inc, K9, inc, K10, inc, K9, inc,

K2, inc, K32[36:40], inc, K2, inc, K9, inc, K10, inc, K9, inc, K2, inc, K10.
__24th row__ P.
__25th row__ K11, inc, K2, inc, K11, inc, K10, inc, K11, inc, K2, inc, K34[38:42], inc, K2, inc, K11, inc, K10, inc, K11, inc, K2, inc, K11.
__26th row__ P.
Continue raglan inc as before, continuing to inc on sleeves at each side of center 10 sts on next 8[9:10] RS rows. 248[264:280] sts.
Work 3[5:7] rows st st inc 8 sts on each RS row for raglan shaping only. 256[280:304] sts.

Dec center sleeve fullness
__Next row__ K21[23:25], inc, K2, inc, K29[32:35], K2 tog, K10, K2 tog tbl, K29 [32:35], inc, K2, inc, K 54[62:70], inc, K2, inc, K29 [32:35], K2 tog, K10, K2 tog tbl, K29[32:35], inc, K2, inc, K21[23:25].
__Next row__ P55[60:65], P2 tog tbl, P10, P2 tog, P122 [136:150], P2 tog tbl, P10, P2 tog, P55[60:65].
Continue inc 8 sts on next 8 RS rows for raglan shaping as before and dec 2 sts on either side of center 10 sts on each sleeve on next 16 rows (RS and WS rows), until there are 256[280:304] sts.

Divide for sleeves
__1st row__ K32[34:36] for left front and slip these sts on holder, **K22[25:28], K2 tog, K10, K2 tog tbl, K22 [25:28], turn.
Work on these sts to complete left sleeve.
Work 3[5:7] rows dec 2 sts on each row on either side of center 10 sts. 50[52:54] sts.
Work 4 rows st st.
Work 4 rows K1, P1 rib.
Change to No.2 needles and work 8 more rows K1, P1 rib. Bind off in rib. **
With RS of work facing, attach yarn to rem sts.
__Next row__ K76[84:92] sts across back and slip sts on holder. Work right sleeve as given for left sleeve working

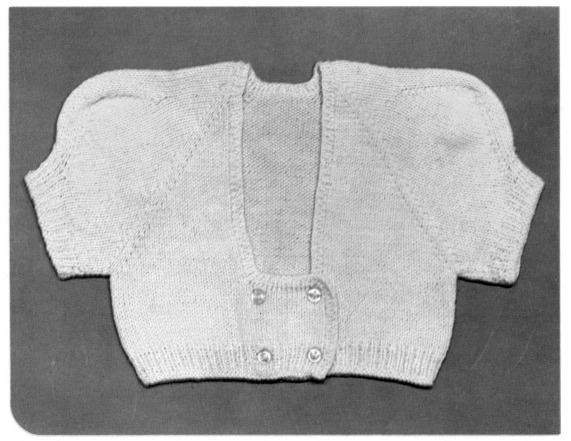

◄ Soft and pretty for spring days

from ** to **.
With RS of work facing,
attach yarn to rem sts for
right front and K32[34:36]
sts.

Next row P32[34:36], P76
[84:92] from back holder and
P32[34:36] from left
front holder.

Next row Cast on 16[20:24]
sts, K across all sts.

Next row Cast on 16[20:24]
sts, P across all sts.
K 1 row. P 1 row.

Next row (buttonhole row)
K to last 16[20:24] sts, bind off
2 sts, K10[14:18] sts, bind off
2 sts, K2.

Next row P2 sts, cast on
2 sts, P10[14:18] sts, cast on
2 sts, P to end.
Work 13[15:17] rows st st.
Change to No.2 needles.
Work 1 row K1, P1 rib.

Next row (buttonhole row)
Rib to last 16[20:24] sts, bind
off 2 sts, rib 10[14:18] sts,
bind off 2 sts, rib 2.

Next row Rib to end, casting
on 2 sts above those bound off
on previous row.
Work 9 more rows K1, P1 rib.
Bind off in rib.

Finishing

Press lightly under a dry
cloth with a cool iron. Join
sleeve seams.
Using No.2 needles, with RS
of work facing, pick up and K
26[28:30] sts from bound-off
edge to top edge of center
front section above buttonholes, 14[18:22] sts along short
cast-on edge above
buttonholes, 56[58:60] sts
along right front edge to
center of raglan shaping
before right sleeve, 40[44:48]
sts evenly around top of
sleeves and back to center of
raglan shaping after left
sleeve, 56[58:60] sts along
left front, 14[18:22] sts from
short cast-on edge of left
center and 26[28:30] sts on
center front edge to lower
bound-off edge. 232[252:272]
sts.
Work 4 rows K1, P1 rib.
Bind off in rib.
Sew buttons in place on left
front to correspond with
buttonholes.

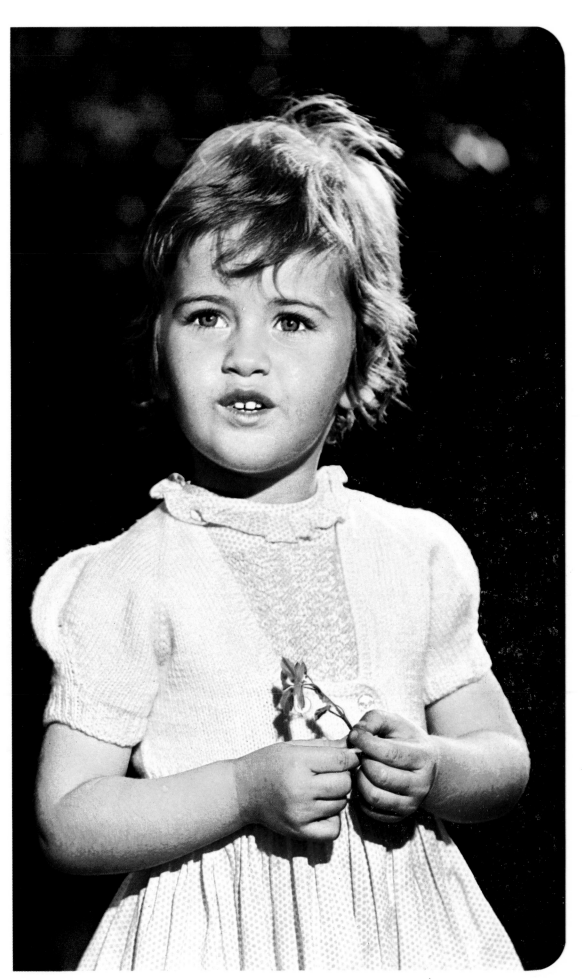

Symmetry in square motifs

Square motifs can be joined together to make various colorful and practical items, such as this afghan.

Size

The afghan is 9 squares wide by 13 squares long, or about 63in by 91in. One square measures approximately 7in.

Gauge

7dc to 2in worked on No.F crochet hook.

Materials

Sports yarn
(2oz skeins)
9 skeins color A, Light Blue
8 skeins color B, Mid-Blue
8 skeins color C, Lime yellow
13 skeins color D, Dark Blue
One No.F (4.00 mm) crochet hook

Note

Each square is worked separately and joined together when all are completed. There are 59 squares worked using D for 1st-3rd rounds, B for 4th-6th rounds and A for 7th-9th rounds, and 58 squares using D for 1st-3rd rounds, C for 4th-6th rounds and D again for 7th-9th rounds.

Square motif

Using No.F crochet hook, ch3. Join with ss to first ch to form circle.

1st round Ch2, work 13dc into circle. Join with ss to 2nd of first 2ch.

2nd round Ch2, 1dc between next 2dc, 2dc between each dc to end. Join with ss to 2nd of first 2ch. 28dc.

3rd round Ch4, skip 2dc, insert hook around next group of 2dc and work 4dc leaving last loop of each dc on hook, yoh and draw through all 5 loops on hook to form cluster—called 1cl—ch1, *1dc between dc of next 2dc group, ch2, 1cl around next 2dc group, ch1, rep from * to end. Join with ss to 2nd of first 4ch.

4th round Change color, joining with ss to first ch sp, ch3, (1dc, ch1) twice into same sp, (1dc, ch1) 3 times into each ch sp to end. Join with ss to 2nd of first 3ch.

5th round Ch3, 1cl around central dc of 3dc group of previous round, ch1, *1dc into sp before next 3dc group, ch1, 1cl around central dc of next 3dc group, ch1, rep from * to end. Join with ss to 2nd of first 3ch.

6th round Ch2, 2dc into first sp, 3dc into each ch sp to end. Join with ss to 2nd of first 2ch.

7th round Change color, joining with ss, ch1, 1sc into each of next 9dc, 1hdc into each of next 3dc, skip 2dc, 5dc into next dc for corner, skip 2dc, 1hdc into each of next 3dc, *1sc into each of next 10dc, 1hdc into each of next 3dc, skip 2dc, 5dc into next dc for corner, skip 2dc, 1hdc into each of next 3dc, rep from * twice more. Join with ss to first ch.

8th round Ch1, 1hdc into each of next 11 sts, 1dc into each of next 2 sts, work 2dc, ch1, 2dc all into corner st, 1dc into each of next 2 sts, *1hdc into each of next 16 sts, 1dc into each of next 2 sts, work 2dc, ch1, 2dc all into corner st, 1dc into each of next 2 sts, rep from * twice more, 1hdc into each of next 4 sts. Join with ss into first ch.

9th round Ch2, 1dc into each of next 15 sts, work 2dc, ch1, 2dc into corner st, *1dc into each of next 23 sts, work 2dc, ch1, 2dc into corner st, rep from * twice more, 1dc into each of next 7 sts. Join with ss to 2nd of first 2ch. Fasten off and darn in all ends.

Finishing

Block and press each square lightly under a damp cloth with a warm iron.
Join squares tog using one row of sc worked on the WS, joining alternate colors.

◄ Detail of the square motif
A useful and colorful afghan ►

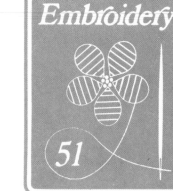

Design in drawn threadwork

Embroidery 51

The stitches shown in this chapter can be adapted to form beautiful modern designs such as the vest, pillows and wall panels illustrated on the following pages.

Drawn threadwork is an interesting form of embroidery based on the removal of either the wrap (lengthwise) or the weft (cross-wise) threads from a precise even-weave fabric. The remaining threads are grouped together into patterns by knotting or interlacing, based on a foundation of ladder hemstitch (see Embroidery chapter 24, page 468).

Each group should contain the same number of threads, usually an even number, so that the threads can be divided evenly when knotting or interlacing to form a pattern.

For an interlaced pattern a large number of threads have to be withdrawn from the fabric to allow sufficient play to form a pattern. The actual number of threads drawn depends greatly on the fabric and thickness of the weave, so it is a good idea to practice on a spare piece of the material before starting the actual work. Avoid withdrawing so many threads that the fabric is weakened.

Fabrics

The best fabrics to use for this technique are even-weave linen or furnishing fabrics of man-made fibers with a precise even weave, such as Dacron. If the fabric weft threads are of a different thickness to the warp threads, the patterns will be distorted and, depending on the thickness of the threads, this will show up in a design to different degrees.

However, if the design is of a free or abstract nature, this uneven-ness of weave can be turned to advantage. The more experienced embroiderer can experiment with unusual and interesting fabrics to create different effects.

For wall hangings, great effect can be achieved with even-weave woolen fabrics, burlap, sacking and the various types of canvas normally used in needlepoint. With canvas an interesting contrast of textures can be achieved by combining drawn threadwork and needlepoint stitches.

Yarns

Traditionally, linen yarns were used for drawn threadwork, but these are no longer easy to obtain. Some extremely interesting results can be achieved with modern threads, however, by using a combination of unusual fabrics and yarns such as gold, silver or copper lurex, weaving yarns or plastic raffia, as well as the more usual yarns such as pearl cotton, embroidery thread, matte embroidery cotton and 6-strand floss. Cords, braids or fine ribbon make attractive interlacings.

Stitches

There are several ways of using the basic foundation of ladder hem-stitch with knotting or interlacing to create different pattern effects.

Four of them are shown here. Zigzag hemstitch (Embroide chapter 24) can also be used as a foundation stitch, but for sor special effects a foundation stitch is not necessary. The results a looser and more open but also less hard-wearing.

Complementary stitches

In modern embroidery almost any combination of stitches is accep able provided the finished result is attractive and does not lo jumbled. Drawn threadwork and needlepoint stitches combi well because they are both worked over counted threads. Ma other filling and line stitches go with drawn threadwork too. F example, rows of drawn threads separated by rows of blocked sat stitch, richly worked spiders' webs or detached eyelets all bui up into instant designs, texture contrasting with the open, lacy loc Stitch Library gives two such complementary stitches.

Color

In drawn threadwork the decoration relies more on texture co trast than color combinations, and the best results come from restricted use of color. Whichever color you choose for the er broidery yarn, be it a lighter or darker tone of the fabric colc an exact match or a complete contrast, use the same color to range throughout. A combination of several contrasting colors yarn simply detracts attention from the design.

Where to use drawn threadwork

Drawn threadwork gives an individual and expensive look household items or clothes—pillows, curtains, wall panels, dress vests, blouses and children's wear. Contrasting ribbon or fabric c. be placed behind the embroidery to dramatize the effect.

Needleweaving

Because the withdrawn threads are replaced by closely wov blocks of stitches, this is a hard-wearing form of the drawn thre. technique.

Woven hemstitch

For the simplest form, withdraw five or six threads. Weave ov the first group of threads (three, four or five, depending on t texture of the fabric—if the fabric is coarse, work over fewe and under the second group. Work back and forth over these tv groups, continuing along the upper half of the threads. The ne block is then worked over the lower half of the second group a the new third group. Pull the weaving firmly so that spaces a left between the blocks. Work with a tapestry needle.

Pyramid border

The needleweaving border is worked over ten groups of threa tapering off to two groups. The number of threads withdrawn a the number in each group depend upon the texture of the fabr

▼ *Woven hemstitch*

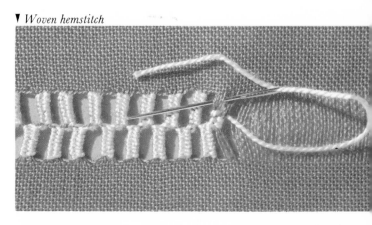

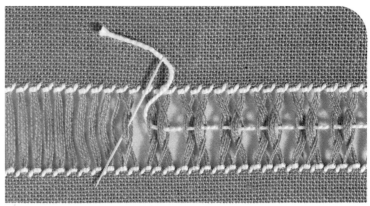

▲ *Interlacing worked over groups of two and four threads*

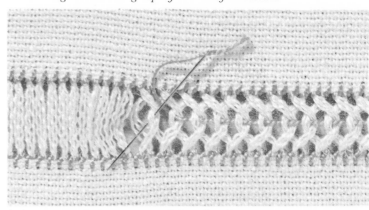

▲ *A pattern worked over groups of three threads*

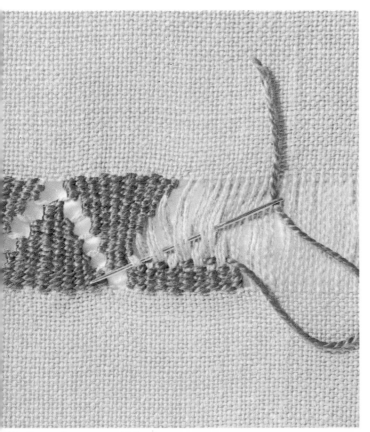

Needleweaving a pyramid border

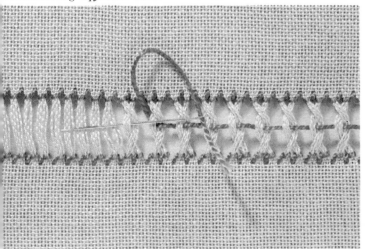

The simplest form of interlacing worked over groups of four threads
Interlacing worked over four groups each of four threads

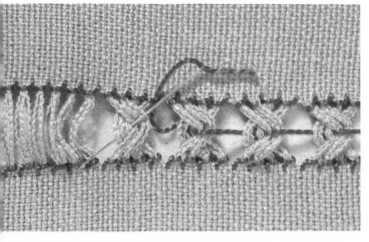

Stitch Library

Rosette chain stitch
This stitch gives a braid effect if worked closely, a petal shape when openly spaced. It can be used in straight or curved lines and is worked from right to left or top to bottom.

Sorbello stitch
This is a knotted stitch which looks best worked in a thick yarn. In a thinner yarn it has a completely different effect. Use it close together as a filling, in single or groups of rows as a border or as a powdering.

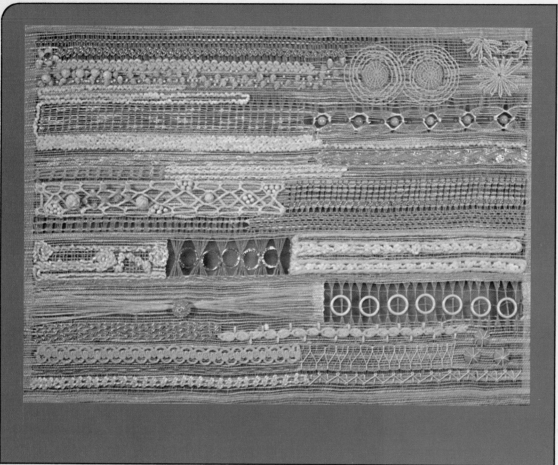

▲ *Abstract panel in the nature of a sampler worked on vision net curtaining fabric*
▼ *A dragonfly worked in a combination of Hardanger embroidery and drawn thread stitches*

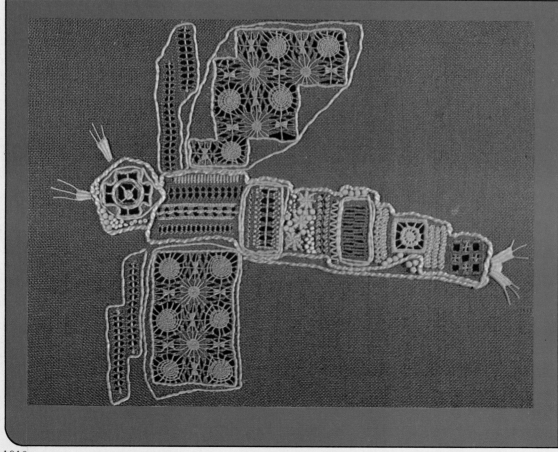

The articles shown on these pages are examples of modern drawn threadwork displaying a variety of textures and the uses to which drawn threadwork can be put.

Abstract panel

This is in the nature of a sampler worked on textured stripes of open-weave vision net curtaining. Some threads have been pulled out giving two very open areas. The rest of the design is a combination of a variety of pulled fabric stitches further decorated with surface stitches such as twisted chain, rosette chain, raised chain band, French knots and couching. Some braids and lamp-shade trimmings have been stitched onto the surface to give a more solid effect. Further texture has been added by using curtain rings, wooden button molds and wooden beads. The sampler is mounted on a contrasting fabric over a wooden frame and measures about 15 inches by 20 inches.

Dragonfly

As the nature of drawn thread-work is to follow the grain of the fabric, the rounded shapes of the insect have been reduced to basic geometric shapes. The design uses a combination of Hardanger embroidery and drawn thread techniques. The design is worked on even-weave linen with threads pulled out for the body stripes which are worked in simple drawn thread stitches. Surface stitches such as raised chain band, woven spider's web and couching for the body outlines give strength and texture to the design. Needle-weaving has also been incorporated using a self color yarn on the body, feelers and tail.

Blue-green pillow

The fabric used is a loosely woven synthetic furnishing tweed which lends itself well to drawn threadwork. The decoration is formed by using small blocks of satin stitch interspersed with large eyelets. The band of withdrawn threads is threaded with narrow, navy blue satin ribbon. The raised decoration and border at each end of the pillow is formed with a row of shell crochet worked in crepe-textured knitting yarn.

Cream pillow

Synthetic curtain fabric with a narrow woven stripe has been used for this pillow. Working from the center outward, the decoration has been formed as follows: The center band of withdrawn threads has been interlaced with two thicknesses of fluffy cotton yarn which has been knotted at regular intervals. Next, a row of square stitch in a broken line is worked using cream pearl cotton. A row of sorbello stitch follows worked in apricot colored pearl cotton. Close to this a row of coral stitch is worked in cream colored matte embroidery cotton.

A row of shaggy weaving cotton follows, couched down, and the next row is knotted stitch in dark cream pearl cotton. The final row of embroidery is pulled satin stitch in broken blocks using dark brown pearl cotton. The border edge is worked in sorbello stitch and pulled satin stitch blocks. The raised bands are rows of shell crochet, which also decorate each end of the pillow.

Vest

The vest is made in cream rayon curtain fabric consisting of stripes of solid and openweave upon which the embroidery design is based.

The panels on either side of the vest are identical. The stitches used, working from the center of each panel outward, are as follows: The center row of stitching is coral knot stitch using thick cream wool worked over the open threads. The next row is raised chain band worked in alternate lengths of crunchy nylon weaving yarn and six strands of floss. The next row is formed with lengths of square stitch and French knots using pearl cotton, Nos. 5 and 8. The outer row is raised chain band worked in thick wool over the open threads of fabric.

▲ *A fashionable vest richly decorated in a variety of simple stitches*
▼ *Detail of stitches on the cream pillow*   ▼ *Detail of stitches on the blue-green pillow*

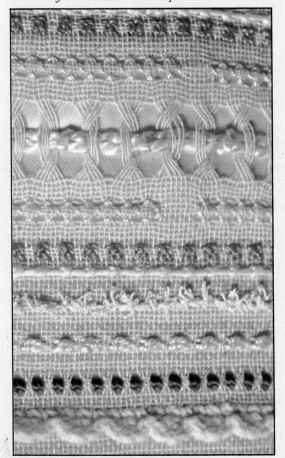

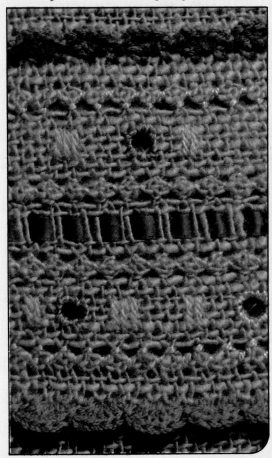

Multiply with many motifs

Many of the basic tatting motifs can be built up into different items so that you can have great fun doing your own designing. If, for instance, you want to make something really ambitious such as a full-size tablecloth and napkins with matching trim, instead of searching for a pattern it becomes a matter of choosing a favorite motif and building it up into an area of the required dimensions.

▼ *The simple, narrow version of the Queen of Hearts border*

The Queen of Hearts border on this page, worked in one or two colors, can easily be made into a deeper border, or by joining several rows you can make a cloth of practically any size desired. At the other extreme, single motifs can be appliquéd or caught through the center to a linen cloth, and a single motif makes a charming insertion for a handkerchief.

Long picots

One new term used in this chapter is the long picot. Simply work a picot in the usual way, but leave a longer space between the two knots so that when closed up a larger picot results.

Queen of Hearts border

This is made in two rows with two shuttles.
1st row. With one shuttle, *make a ring of 8ds, 1 long p, 8ds, close. Reverse work.
With two shuttles, ch of 5ds, 1p, 4ds, 1 Josephine knot, 4ds, 1p, 5ds, reverse work.
With one shuttle, make a ring of 8ds, join to long p of previous ring, 8ds, close *.
Repeat from * to * to the required length; then, with two shuttles, work the turn at the end of the row with ch of 5ds, 5p separated by 2ds, 5ds, reverse work.
2nd row. Work as before, back along the first row, joining two rings to each of the long picots. When back at the beginning, finish off with a ch of 5ds, 5p separated by 2ds, 5ds. Cut and tie the ends to the beginning of the border and finish off by threading the ends neatly into the work.

Double Queen of Hearts border

Work as for narrow border, but on the second row work picots instead of Josephine knots. Finish off the thread.
3rd row. Work as for first row, omitting Josephine knots and joining instead to the middle picots on the chains of the second row.
4th row. Work as for second row of narrow border.

Tray cloth or tablecloth

Continue as for the double border, remembering to work Josephine knots only on the first and last rows, substituting joining picots on the rows in between.

Single motifs

Work from * to * of first row once, reverse work and make turning with ch of 5ds, 5p separated by 2ds, 5ds. Reverse work and repeat from * to * once more, joining rings at center, reverse work and make a further turning ch. Cut and tie ends to beginning and finish off by threading the ends into the work.

Diadem motif

This is worked with two shuttles and consists of a series of scallops. Begin at the center of the lower edge.
With one shuttle, make a ring of 10ds, 1p, 10ds, close. Reverse work.
With two shuttles, ch of 6ds, 1p, 6ds.
With one shuttle, ring of 4ds, 1p, 4ds, 1p, 4ds, 1p, 4ds, close. Make another ring of 4ds, join to last p of previous ring, 4ds, 1p, 4ds, 1p, 4ds, close. Reverse work.
With two shuttles, ch of 8ds, join to p of first ring, reverse work.
With one shuttle, ring of 4ds, join to last p of previous ring, 4ds, 1p, 4ds, 1p, 4ds, close. Reverse work.
With two shuttles, ch of 10ds, reverse work.

Diadem motif border and ▼ *Butterfly and flower motif border, both of which could be built up in rows by reversing or interlocking*

With one shuttle, ring of 4ds, join to last p of previous ring, 4ds, 1p, 4ds, 1p, 4ds, close. Repeat two more rings in the same way to form a trefoil, reverse work.

With two shuttles, ch of 10ds, reverse work.

With one shuttle, ring of 4ds, join to last p of previous ring, 4ds, 1p, 4ds, 1p, 4ds, close. Reverse work.

With two shuttles, ch of 8ds, reverse work.

With one shuttle, ring of 4ds, join to last p of previous ring, 4ds, 1p, 4ds, 1p, 4ds, close. Make another ring of 4ds, join to last p of previous ring, 4ds, 1p, 4ds, 1p, 4ds, close.

With two shuttles, ch of 6ds, 1p, 6ds, reverse work.

With one shuttle, ring of 10ds, join to intersection of fourth and fifth chains, 10ds, close.

Cut and tie ends of beginning of motif and run the ends into the work. This completes one scallop.

Make others in the same way, joining at the second p of the corner base ring to the equivalent point of the previous scallop.

Butterfly and flower motif

This is made in one row with two shuttles and works from left to right.

With one shuttle, make a ring of 8ds, 1 long p, 8ds, close *. Reverse work.

With two shuttles, ch of 6ds, 1p, 6ds, reverse work.

With one shuttle, make a second ring of 8ds, join to long p of first ring, 8ds, close *.

Repeat from * to * three times more.

With two shuttles, ch of 5ds, 1p, 3ds, 1p, 3ds, 1p, 5ds, reverse work.

With one shuttle, ring of 4ds, join to p of second to the last chain, 4ds, 1p, 4ds, 1p, 4ds, close. Reverse work.

With two shuttles, ch of 5ds, 1p, 3ds, 1p, 3ds, 1p, 5ds.

Repeat from the beginning, joining the first chain to the last ring as shown.

Make a Polly wool doll

Make this lovely little lady, Polly by name, from braided wool. A ping-pong ball is used for her head, giving it a nice rounded shape, and when completed she is about 10 inches long. Instructions are given here for making her a gingham dress with pantaloons.

You will need:

- ☐ 2oz white sports yarn
- ☐ ½oz black sports yarn
- ☐ A ping-pong ball
- ☐ Rubber cement
- ☐ Scraps of red and green felt
- ☐ 1yd 1in wide pink ribbon
- ☐ ¼yd 36in wide gingham fabric
- ☐ 1½yd 1in wide eyelet embroidery trimming
- ☐ Matching threads, basting thread
- ☐ Sewing needle, darning needle
- ☐ 3 small snap fasteners
- ☐ ½yd each shirring elastic, ¼in wide elastic

Making the doll

The arms. First cut two 10 inch lengths of white yarn and put them aside for binding the arms.

Then make a skein from the white yarn about 12 inches long and 60 strands thick. Cut the skein at each end and bind it firmly with one of the 10 inch lengths of white yarn about 1 inch from one end (figure **1**).

1

Braid the skein and bind the braid 1 inch from the other end with the other 10 inch length of yarn (figure **2**).

2

The body and legs. Prepare five 10 inch lengths of white yarn for binding the body and legs. Make a skein from the white yarn about 30 inches long and 80 strands thick, cut the skein at each end and bind it firmly in the middle (figure **3**).

3

Lay the arms across the middle of the skein, fold the skein over them, then bind it firmly just below the arms to hold them in place (figure **4**).
Bind the skein again about 1 inch farther down to make the waist. From this point divide the skein in half and braid each half to make the legs. Bind each leg firmly 1 inch from each end as shown in figure **4**.
Trim the ends of the arms and legs into a neat shape.
The head. Cover the ping-pong ball with rubber cement, leaving a small space at the top and bottom so you can hold it between your thumb and forefinger.
Wind white yarn around and around the ping-pong ball being careful that all the strands go in the same direction and

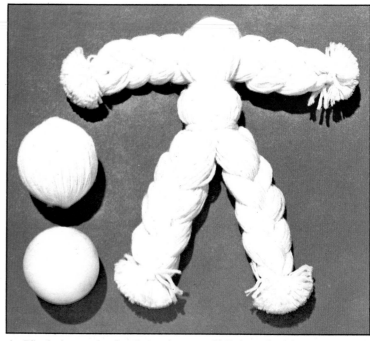

4. *The body completed and the ping-pong ball covered with yarn*

cross at the top and bottom (see figure **4**). When the ping-pong ball is completely covered, darn in the loose end of the yarn to make it neat.
Leave the head to dry completely.
Thread the darning needle with white yarn and sew the head to the body.
The face. Cut two circles from the green felt, about ½ inch in diameter for the eyes. Cut an oval from the red felt, about ¾ inch across and 2 tiny circles for the mouth and nose. Stick the eyes, nose and mouth to the head using a little cement and then, using matching thread, sew the features down with neat blanket stitches around the edges.
The hair. Cut forty 8 inch lengths of black yarn and sew them to the top of the head (figure **5**). Sew through the

5

center of each strand, letting the ends hang down around the head.
Trim bangs at the front and sew the strands down at the back of the head to secure them.

Divide the hair into bunches and tie them with bows of pink ribbon.

Making the dress and pantaloons

The dress. From the gingham measure and cut a strip 12 inches long and 5 inches wide for the skirt, and two 3 inch squares for the bodice.
Fold the skirt strip in half, right sides facing, and stitch the two short edges together using a ½ inch seam allowance. Press the seam open.
Make a ½ inch turned hem on one of the edges of the skirt and then sew eyelet embroidery trimming to the hemmed edge (figure **6**).
Take one of the bodice squares and cut it in half for the back.
Place the back halves and front bodice together, right sides facing, and stitch the side and shoulder seams as shown in figure **7**, using a ½ inch seam allowance. Press the seams open and neatly hem the center back opening, armhole and

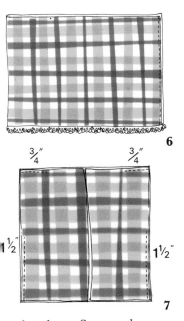

6

7

neck edges. Sew eyelet embroidery trimming around the neck and armholes (figure **8**) and sew three snap fasteners down the center back opening.

8

Gather up the raw edge of the skirt to fit the bodice at the waist. Baste eyelet embroidery along the gathered waist edge on the right side of the skirt. With right sides facing, place the seam of the skirt to the center back opening of the bodice and stitch the bodice and skirt together, taking a ½ inch seam.

Overcast the raw seam edges together to finish them.

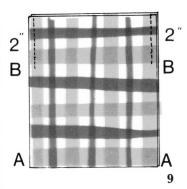

9

▲ *Polly wool doll dressed in all her finery*

The pantaloons. From the remaining gingham, measure and cut two pieces 6 inches long and 5 inches wide. Place the pieces together, right sides facing, and stitch them together as shown in figure **9**, taking a ½ inch seam.

Fold the pantaloons so that the seams are at the center back and center front and stitch the legs as shown in figure **10**, from **A** to **B** to **A.** Make a ½ inch turned hem at the bottom of each leg and sew eyelet embroidery trimming to the hem-

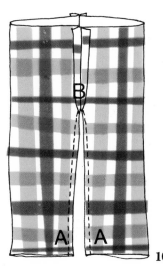

10

med edges.

Make a ½ inch turned hem at the waist edge, leaving a small opening. Insert ¼in wide elastic through the opening and draw up the elastic to fit the doll's waist. Secure the elastic and close the opening with slip stitch.

Thread the darning needle with shirring elastic and make a row of running stitches 1 inch above the trimmed edge of each leg. This will draw up the legs of the pantaloons to make frills.

The tailored knit look

Dresses made in knits are very comfortable, easy to wear, allow complete freedom of movement and, if made from a man-made fiber knit, are also extremely practical because they wash well—in fact, many of the man-made knits do not even need an iron to smooth them out after washing. In addition, some of the double knits, such as polyester, are so hard wearing that they are almost indestructible and still look like new after many, many washings.

This chapter gives hints on sewing knits and how to fit garments made in this fabric. Because knit has natural stretch, the knitting is a most important feature.

The dress illustrated here, with its smooth lines and long fitted sleeves, is an ideal style for knits, which in this particular case is a double knit pure wool jersey with a fine, stockinette stitch surface. This knit handles very well in all stages of making the pattern.

The dress is an adaptation of the basic dress pattern from the Creative Hands Pattern Pack and you can make it from the instructions given in this chapter. These are special instructions for fitting and making garments made in knit, and you will find them invaluable for other styles too.

Details of the dress include a loose lining which is stitched into the neckline with the facing and into the armhole seams. Since there is a natural give in knit the long, fitted sleeves can be closely fitted and then finished with a zipper opening at each wrist edge.

About knits

Types of knits

Knit fabrics are made in a variety of textures. Starting with the plain, printed or jacquard knits, there is the honeycomb finish and the stockinette stitch finish. Generally the honeycomb surface is found on the heavier and coarser knits and the stockinette stitch surface on the finer ones. But both finishes come in double or single knits.

Then there are knits with a raised surface pattern resembling a cloqué. These are usually in man-made fabrics where the resilience of the fiber helps to retain the pattern shape on the surface. These are found mostly in double knits.

Added to the difference in texture is the fact that knits are now made in many different fibers, both natural and man-made. You will find that each knit has different characteristics, so that when shopping for a knit fabric you will have to keep the style of the garment you are making in mind. Once it could be assumed that knits only lent themselves to a particular style; this is no longer true and knits can be used for tailored designs as well as for the more molded, draped or figure-hugging ones. Be sure to choose the correct texture for the style you want to make.

Don't forget to find out whether the fabric should be washed or dry cleaned when you buy it.

The tailored knit look

Although all knits will mold well to the figure, the heavier ones are most successfully used for really tailored and sculptured styles. They give you freedom of movement and a crisp looking garment without bulk, and contrary to what you may expect, it does not take a clever dressmaker to combine all these qualities in one garment.

Stitching knits

Since knit fabric spreads when under pressure, reduce the pressure on the presser foot of the machine.

Use the finest needle size possible on the machine or one of the new ball-point needles and a thickness of thread to suit the needle size.

To stitch the seams, engage the smallest zigzag stitch setting plus a stitch length setting of 12 to 14 stitches per inch. Then, as you are stitching, stretch the seams very gently to give the maximum elasticity to the zigzag stitches.

Seams which have to withstand a lot of strain, such as the Center Back and armhole seams, should be stitched over twice.

If the machine is missing stitches as you stitch the seams, and this often happens when stitching knits, it usually means that the combination of needle and thread is wrong. However, if your machine is very light, it may mean that the fabric is too heavy for the machine to cope with.

Curved seams in knits

The curved seams in knits do not usually need snipping if the seam allowance is narrow, that is $\frac{1}{2}$ to $\frac{3}{4}$ inch. But if you have found a fabric which rolls and does not mold easily, then snip the seam allowance to not less than $\frac{1}{4}$ inch from the stitching line.

Finishing raw edges in knits

Although the inside of a dress looks better when the raw edges of the seam allowances are finished, it is not necessary to finish knit because it does not fray. But if you want to apply a seam edge finish, make sure it is very flat and does not create a thick ridge which would make an impression through the fabric to the outside of the garment.

Zippers in knits

When inserting a zipper into the Center Back of a knit dress, make the opening 1 inch longer than the zipper to allow for the $\frac{1}{2}$ inch distance from neck stitching line and $\frac{1}{2}$ inch for ease. If you find that the opening has dropped when you begin to insert the zipper, it will be safe to ease in the surplus.

With some knits you may have to pin in the zipper and hold the dress up to see if the fabric drops away in folds. If it does, keep repinning until the folds have disappeared. It does not help to tape the opening as you will still have the same problem.

Fortunately, most double knits will take a zipper without any problems at all.

Fitting

Knit fabrics need special and careful fitting, and it is well worthwhile reading the fitting instructions for the knit garment even if you don't intend to make this particular version.

The dress pattern, yardage and notions

The pattern pieces

For this dress you need five pattern pieces: the Front, Back, long fitted sleeve, front neck facing and back neck facing.

Front and Back patterns. Copy the Front and Back pattern pieces from the basic dress sheet in the Creative Hands Pattern Pack, numbers 1 and 2, incorporating any corrections you may have made previously for figure faults. Do not cut them out yet.

The dress is made with a Center Back opening and a Center Front seam, so mark both for seaming.

As with all knit fabrics, avoid darts as much as possible and do not use the body darts. Although the dress is semi-fitted, the ease is taken into the seams and the side bust darts instead.

The Center Front and Center Back seams are slightly curved through the waistline (figures **1** and **2**). So first mark in your waistline on the Front and Back pattern pieces and then curve the center seams as follows.

For the Front, measure $\frac{3}{8}$ inch from the Center Front at the waistline and taper into the original Center Front top and bottom (figure 1). Curve the Center Back in the same way, but measure in $\frac{3}{4}$ inch at the waistline (figure **2**).

Slant the side bust dart on the dress Front downward by $1\frac{1}{2}$ inches at the outer end, leaving the point of the dart where it is (figure 1). This will help to take in some of the fullness at the waistline of the dress.

When you have moved the dart, make sure that you compensate on the side seams as shown, so that the seamlines of the upper and lower stitching lines are the same length.

Do not deepen the dart or curve the waistline at the side seams yet. This is done more accurately at the fitting stage.

Front and back facing patterns. Using the Front and Back pattern pieces copy the relevant top sections of each (figures **1** and **2**) and make the front and back neck facings as shown. They are 2 inches wide and should be trimmed shorter at the shoulder by $\frac{1}{8}$ inch (figure **3**). Mark the Center Front on the front facing pattern to be cut on the fold.

Sleeve pattern. Use the sleeve pattern piece number 7 from the accessory sheet in the Pattern Pack.

Cut out all the pattern pieces.

Layouts and yardages

Dressmaking 46, page 916, explains the process of making layouts and finding the minimum yardage requirements. As knit fabrics are available in 36 inch to 72 inch widths, it is helpful to know the width you intend to buy to save yourself making trial layouts for 36, 48, 54, 60 and 72 inch widths to work out the required yardage!

Before making a trial layout here are a few points to note:

The facings are very small and can be cut from the scraps.

The seam and hem allowances are not included in the Creative Hands patterns so you will need to add $\frac{3}{4}$ inch for seams and $2\frac{1}{2}$ inches for hems.

The hem allowance on the long fitted sleeve should be $2\frac{1}{2}$ inches so that you can adjust the length at the fitting.

If you are using knit with a heavy drop, such as a rayon jersey, allow plenty of margin between the pattern pieces on the layout since it is advisable to cut slightly wider seam allowances. Garments in these fabrics often require a little more ease because they fall so close to the body.

To start you off on your layout, here is a guide for the yardage requirements for 36, 54 and 72 inch widths. Measure out the amounts and work from there.

36 inch width. For standard sizes, start with twice the dress length plus one sleeve length plus hem and seam allowances.

Large sizes may have to be cut on an open layout when it becomes necessary to add one more dress length for safety.

54 inch width. For standard sizes start with one dress length plus

The long sleeved dress version made in a double knit wool jersey►

one sleeve length plus hem and seam allowances.

For large sizes the pattern pieces may have to be staggered and may require up to half a dress length extra.

72 inch width. One dress length plus hem and seam allowances should be sufficient for all sizes.

Lining. Only the Back and Front of the dress are cut from lining fabric. The sleeves are not lined, nor are the facings.

Notions
- [ ] One 24 inch zipper for the Center Back
- [ ] Two 5 inch zippers for the sleeves (optional)
- [ ] One hook, size no. 1
- [ ] Fine machine or ball-point needles
- [ ] Matching thread

Cutting out and marking pattern details
Cut out the knit fabric adding hem and seam allowances.

Mark the pattern detail with a fine soft thread, such as a number 50 basting thread sold for this purpose. A sharp thread can cut the knit stitches, resulting in nasty runs.

Fitting knit fabrics

When making a knit dress fitting stages are very important. There are three fitting stages. The first is with the body of the dress semi-basted. The second fitting stage is with the body of the dress completely basted to include corrections made in the first stage.

The third stage is the final check with zipper, lining and sleeves basted in position. If you make any alterations at this stage, then try it on finally to see that all is well.

Preparing for the first fitting
Pin and baste the shoulder darts if used.

Pin the side bust darts but do not baste them.

Pin and baste the Center Front seam, and the Center Back seam from the end of the opening to the hem.

Pin and baste the shoulder seams.

Pin the side seams and baste them from underarm to dart and from waist to hem.

Do not press at this stage, as for other fabrics.

Before you slip on the dress, remove the pins from the darts and that section of each side seam which has not been basted.

The first fitting
It is best to do this fitting with the help of two mirrors so that you can see the back as well as the front.

Fit the side bust darts first, by taking the lower dart stitching line and folding it toward the upper dart stitching line. You will then see how much more fabric you can take into the dart to get rid of the fullness above the waistline. Roll the surplus fabric into the dart by rolling the lower dart stitching line under until the front looks smooth (figure **4**).

Deepening the darts does not mean that you take any more depth into the ends of the darts where they go into the side seams (see figure **4**). You only do this when you have to pin off a lot of surplus fabric into the side seams—and this is the next stage.

Now stand relaxed in front of the mirror with both arms beside the body. The area above the waistline should look perfectly smooth without fitting too snugly to the body. There should be no upward drag lines toward the darts. If there are, it means that you have taken in the darts too far down the stitching line and they must be let out.

The remaining fullness in the dress must now be pinned off at the

side seams by deepening the curve through the waistline and over the hips.

Now fit the back of the dress.

If pinning fullness into the side seams causes the dress to pull into the waistline and toward the sides at the back, unpin some fullness from the side seams on the dress Back only and deepen the Center Back seam curve until the back hangs smoothly.

The Center Back and Center Front should not, however, be fitted too closely to the figure, but should fall into a softly molding line.

The second fitting
Correct all the fitting faults from the first fitting and mark them on the pattern ready to cut the lining for the third fitting. Then baste the dress as corrected and try it on, making any small alterations that may be necessary.

Preparing for the third fitting
Stitch and press all darts and seams in the dress. The darts should be slashed along the centers and pressed open and the seam allowances reduced to $\frac{5}{8}$ inch, or less in the case of the shoulder darts. To obtain a perfect molding at the points of the side bust darts, press them carefully over the rounded end of a pressing ham.

If you wish to overcast the seam edges, do so now but omit the shoulder seam edges.

Press the Center Back opening seam allowances as fitted and pin and baste in the zipper.

Make the lining as for the dress. The darts are stitched on the outside of the fabric, that is, the side of the lining which goes to the body. This will prevent the thickness of the darts from making an impression on the knit fabric. The seams are stitched on the inside of the lining as usual.

Finish the seams of the lining as flat as possible so that they will not show through. Trim the shoulder seams to $\frac{1}{2}$ inch but do not overcast them.

Pin and baste the lining to the dress around the neckline and armhole seams (figure **5**). The lining will be caught into the armhole seams when the sleeves are stitched in. This secures the shoulderline as in some knits fitted sleeves can cause the shoulder seams to drop.

Pin and baste the sleeve seams, leaving 5 inches open at each wrist end for the zipper opening if you intend to make the sleeves really fitted.

Pin and baste the sleeves into the armholes.

The third fitting
Slip on the dress and close the zipper.

Check the sleeve fitting around the armholes and over the shoulders, then fit the sleeves as follows.

Pin the sleeve openings together and fit the sleeves close to the forearm as far as the elbow. If you want to dispense with the zippers, make each wrist edge just wide enough to enable you to push your hand through.

The upper arm area of the sleeves should be close fitting but not tight, so move your arms up and down to make sure that the seams will not break. All long fitted sleeves restrain your movement somewhat, even in knits, but you must sacrifice some freedom for style. Long fitted sleeves must always be made a little longer than other sleeves as they have a tendency to ride up on the arms and look too short if made the usual length. The extra length is only needed if you are fitting the sleeves closely.

Check the length of the dress, and trim the excess hem allowance on the sleeves to make a 1 to $\frac{3}{4}$ inch hem.

Finally check the back fitting of the dress once more, especially around the zipper area. The zipper should lie flat and the fabric around it should not bulge, nor should it be held in too tightly.

Finishing the dress

Zipper and facing. Stitch in the zipper.

Stitch the front neck facing to the back neck facing at the shoulder seams. Trim the seam allowance, then pin and baste the facing to the neck edge of the dress, right sides together, pinning the ends of the zipper tape out of the way.

Stitch the facing to the dress around the neck edge and trim the seam allowance.

Snip into the seam allowance of the lining at short intervals. The seam allowance of the knit fabric may also have to be snipped if it does not lie easily. But before deciding to snip the knit fabric, first turn the facing to the inside and edge-baste and press it to see how much resistance there is on the seam edge.

Turn in the raw edges of the lining clear of the zipper teeth down the Center Back opening and hand sew to the zipper tape. Then fold in the ends of the back neck facing to clear the zipper teeth and sew to the tape.

Sew the facing to the lining with long slip stitches.

Press the top edge of the opening and close with a hand-worked bar and a small hook.

Sleeves. Finish the sleeve openings before stitching the sleeves into the armholes. If you are not putting zippers in the openings, finish the sleeve hems in the usual way. Otherwise stitch in the zippers and make the hems as shown (figure **6**), mitering the ends of each hem over the ends of the zipper tape.

Finally stitch the sleeves, trim the seam allowance of the armholes and overcast to finish (see Dressmaking 37, figure **7**, page 738).

Hem. When finishing the hem, use the invisible catch stitch as shown in Dressmaking chapter 12, page 236. This gives extra strength and allows the stitches to give with the fabric.

Turn up the lining hem 1 inch shorter than the dress and machine stitch or hem in place.

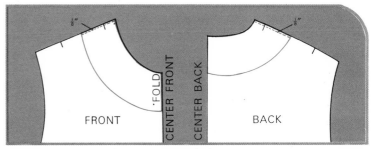

▲ **3.** *The trimmed front and back neck facings*
▼ **4.** *Deepening the side bust dart*

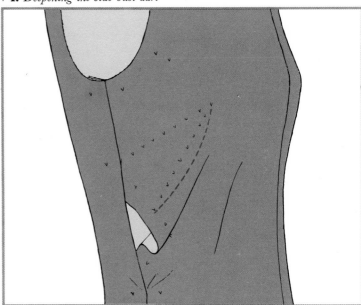

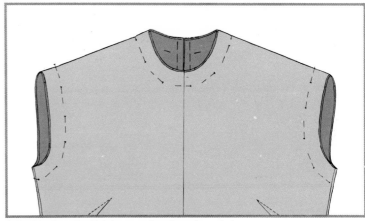

▲ **5.** *Pinning the lining around neck and armholes*
▼ **6.** *The sleeve hem with zipper fastening*

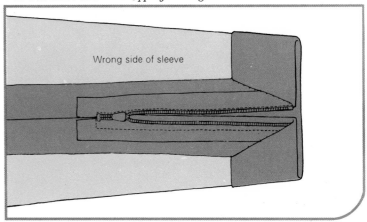

▼ **1.** *The dress Front pattern*

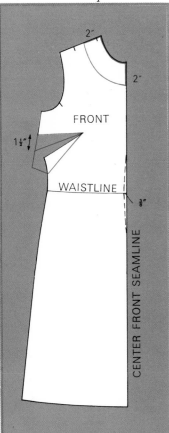

▼ **2.** *The dress Back pattern*

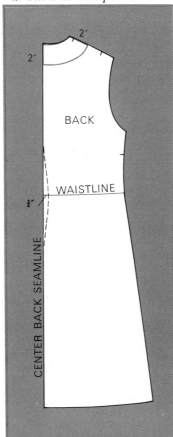

Fashion Flair

Japanese flowers

Stylized flowers make ideal motifs for appliqué or various embroidery techniques.

1. *A pretty idea for a hostess apron—use the motifs in appliqué and make a cut work border.*

2. *Embroider the motifs into exotic blooms to decorate a kimono-style dress or robe.*

Creative hint *Work a motif on organdy or semi-transparent fabric, making it firm with a satin stitch or buttonhole stitch outline; cut out the shape and hang in a window. Seen against the light this creates a pretty snowflake effect which is very popular in the Scandinavian countries.*

Pattern Library

Pineapple motif

This interesting interpretation of a pineapple is worked in a variety of stitches and gay colors. The yarn used here is matte embroidery cotton in closely related tones of pinks, violets and browns with a contrasting green.

The stitches are chain stitch, outline stitch, satin stitch, seeding and running stitch.

Use the motif on home furnishings or beach wear.

More about Aran stitches

Stitches in cables and twisted panels which form many Aran patterns may change their position, but they usually return to their original place in the pattern sequence within a few rows. Traveling stitches, on the other hand, may move on every row or alternate row throughout the entire pattern repeat and form the basis of all trellis and lattice patterns, as well as being used in single motifs such as Tree of Life pattern and Marriage Lines pattern.

A simplified form of trellis stitch, where only one ridge travels in a zigzag pattern within a panel, symbolizes the ups and downs of married life. Using a double ridge, a diamond pattern is formed (see the man's cardigan featured in Basic Wardrobe 41, p. 804). This is often used as an all-over design and is reminiscent of the small walled fields of Ireland. The pattern also means "wealth." Extra texture may be added by filling the center of each diamond with seed stitch, trinity stitch, or rock-like bobbles.
Narrow lines of traveling stitches branching out from a central stem form the famous Tree of Life design, sometimes used inverted with the branches drooping instead of rising upward.

Trellis sampler

The sampler is edged with a narrow panel of twisted stitches and is ideal for working in strips, which can then be joined together to make pillows, afghans or bedspreads.
Worked over 58 stitches.
1st row. K1, P1, K1 putting yarn twice around needle—called K1y2rn—K2, P2, K1, P3, (sl 2 sts onto cable needle and hold at back of work, K2, K2 from cable needle—called C4B—P4) 4 times, C4B, P3, K1, P2, K1y2rn, K2, P1, K1.
2nd row. K2, P2, sl 1 dropping extra loop and keeping yarn on WS, K2, P1, K2, (P4, K4) 3 times, P4, K3, P1, K2, P2, sl 1 dropping extra loop and keeping yarn on WS, K2.
3rd row. K1, P1, sl next st onto cable needle and hold at front of work, K1y2rn, K1, K1 from cable needle—called CTw3—P2, K1, P2, (sl next st onto cable needle and hold at back of work, K2, P1 from cable needle—called C3PB—sl next 2 sts onto cable needle and hold at front of work, P1, K2 from cable needle—called C3PF—P2) 5 times, K1, P2, CTw3, P1, K1.
4th row. K2, P2, sl 1, K2, P1, K2, (P2, K2) 10 times, P1, K2, P2, sl 1, K2.
5th row. K1, P1, CTw3, P2, K1, P1, (C3PB, P2, C3PF) 5 times, P1, K1, P2, CTw3, P1, K1.
6th row. K2, P2, sl 1, K2, P1, K1, (P2, K4, P2) 5 times, K1, P1, K2, P2, sl 1, K2.
7th row. K1, P1, CTw3, P2, K1, P1, K2, P4, (sl next 2 sts onto cable needle and hold at front of work, K2, K2 from cable needle —called C4F—P4) 4 times, K2, P1, K1, P2, CTw3, P1, K1.
8th row. K2, P2, sl 1, K2, P1, K1, (P2, K4, P2) 5 times, K1, P1, K2, P2, sl 1, K2.

9th row. K1, P1, CTw3, P2, K1, P1, (C3PF, P2, C3PB) 5 times, P1, K1, P2, CTw3, P1, K1.
10th row. K2, P2, sl 1, K2, P1, K1, (K1, P2, K1) 10 times, K1, P1, K2, P2, sl 1, K2.·
11th row. K1, P1, CTw3, P2, K1, P2, (C3PF, C3PB, P2) 5 times, K1, P2, CTw3, P1, K1.
12th row. K2, P2, sl 1, K2, P1, K1, (K2, P4, K2) 5 times, K1, P1, K2, P2, sl 1, K2.
13th row. K1, P1, CTw3, P2, K1, P3, (C4B, P4) 4 times, C4B, P3, K1, P2, CTw3, K2, P1, K1.
Rows 2-13 form pattern and are repeated throughout.

Bobble sampler

This sampler is also edged and can be used in combination with the trellis sampler to produce a textured fabric.
Worked over 47 stitches.
1st row. (RS) K1, P1, K1y2rn, K2, P3, K1, P2, *into next st work K1, P1, K1, P1, K1 making 5 sts out of 1, turn and K these 5 sts, turn and P these 5 sts, lift 4th st over 5th and off needle and rep with 3rd, 2nd and 1st st until one st rems—called bobble 1—P5, rep from * to last 12 sts, bobble 1, P2, K1, P3, K1y2rn, K2, P1, K1.
2nd row. K2, P2, sl 1 dropping extra loop and keeping yarn on WS, K3, P1, K29, P1, K3, P2, sl 1, K2.
3rd row. K1, P1, sl next st onto cable needle and hold at front of work, K1y2rn, K1, K1 from cable needle—called CTw3—P3, K1, P29, K1, P3, CTw3, P1, K1.
4th row. As 2nd row.
5th row. K1, P1, CTw3, P3, K1, *P5, bobble 1, rep from * to last 14 sts, P5, K1, P3, CTw3, P1, K1.
6th row. As 2nd row.
7th row. As 3rd row.
8th row. As 2nd row.
9th row. K1, P1, CTw3, P3, K1, P2, *bobble 1, P5, rep from * to last 12 sts, bobble 1, P2, K1, P3, CTw3, P1, K1.
Rows 2-9 form pattern and are repeated throughout.

Tree of Life

Worked over a number of stitches divisible by 15.
1st row. (RS) *P7, K1, P7, rep from * to end.
2nd row. *K7, P1, K7, rep from * to end.
3rd row. *P5, slip next st onto cable needle and hold at back, K1, P1 from cable needle—called C2F—K1, slip next st onto cable needle and hold at front, P1, K1, from cable needle—called C2B—P5, rep from * to end.
4th row. *K5, sl 1 keeping yarn on WS, K1, P1, K1, sl 1, K5, rep from * to end.
5th row. *P4, C2F, P1, K1, P1, C2B, P4, rep from * to end.
6th row. *K4, sl 1, K2, P1, K2, sl 1, K4, rep from * to end.
7th row. *P3, C2F, P2, K1, P2, C2B, P3, rep from * to end.
8th row. *K3, sl 1, K3, P1, K3, sl 1, K3, rep from * to end.
9th row. *P2, C2F, P3, K1, P3, C2B, P2, rep from * to end.
10th row. *K2, sl 1, K4, P1, K4, sl 1, K2, rep from * to end.
These 10 rows form pattern and are repeated throughout.

Marriage lines

Worked over a number of stitches divisible by 20.
1st row. *P1, Tw2F, P6, K2, P2, K2, P2, Tw2B, P1, rep from * to end.
2nd row. *K1, P2, K2, P2, K2, P2, K6, P2, K1, rep from * to end.
3rd row. *P1, Tw2F, P5, sl next st onto cable needle and hold at back of work, K2, P1 from cable needle—called T3R—P1, T3R, P2, Tw2B, P1, rep from * to end.
4th row. *K1, P2, K3, P2, K2, P2, K5, P2, K1, rep from * to end.
5th row. *P1, Tw2F, P4, T3R, P1, T3R, P3, Tw2B, P1, rep from * to end.

▲ *Trellis sampler edged with twisted stitch panel*

▲ *Bobble sampler edged with twisted stitch panel*

▲ *Tree of Life pattern*

▲ *Marriage lines pattern with twisted stitch panels*

6th row. *K1, P2, K4, P2, K2, P2, K4, P2, K1, rep from * to end.

7th row. *P1, Tw2F, P3, T3R, P1, T3R, P4, Tw2B, P1, rep from * to end.

8th row. *K1, P2, K5, P2, K2, P2, K3, P2, K1 rep from * to end.

9th row. *P1, Tw2F, P2, T3R, P1, T3R, P5, Tw2B, P1, rep from * to end.

10th row. *K1, P2, K6, P2, K2, P2, K2, P2, K1, rep from * to end.

11th row. *P1, Tw2F, P2, sl next 2 sts onto cable needle and hold at front of work, P1, K2 from cable needle—called T3L—P1, T3L, P5, Tw2B, P1, rep from * to end.

12th row. As 8th row.

13th row. *P1, Tw2F, P3, T3L, P1, T3L, P4, Tw2B, P1, rep from * to end.

14th row. As 6th row.

15th row. *P1, Tw2F, P4, T3L, P1, T3L, P3, Tw2B, P1, rep from * to end.

16th row. As 4th row.

17th row. *P1, Tw2F, P5, T3L, P1, T3L, P2, Tw2B, P1, rep from * to end.

Rows 2-17 form pattern and are repeated throughout.

Knitted coat for a beautiful bride

This superb design represents all that is best in hand knitting. Shown here as an exquisite bridal coat, the same pattern would make an evening coat if it were knitted in a bright colored yarn. Alternatively, by carrying the button loop fastening down to the hem, the coat would make an elegant coat-dress for evening occasions. The hood is optional and can be omitted, leaving a mandarin collar. The pearl trim is optional.

Size

Directions are for 34-36in bust with 36-38in hips. Length from center back, 58in. Sleeve seam, 18in.

Gauge

7 sts and 9 rows to 1in over stockinette stitch worked on No.3 needles.

Gauge for this pattern

7½ sts and 9 rows to 1in over patt worked on No.3 needles.

Materials

3-ply fingering yarn (1oz skeins)
Coat 19 skeins
Hood 2 skeins
One pair No.3 needles (or Canadian No. 10)
One No.D (3.00 mm) crochet hook
70 pearls (optional)

Back

Using No.3 needles, cast on 250 sts.

1st row K1, P8, *K6, ytf, sl 1, K2 tog, psso, ytf, K6, P16, rep from * ending P8, K1 instead of P16.

2nd and every other row K9, *P15, K16, rep from * ending K9 instead of K16.

3rd row As 1st.

5th row As 1st.

7th row As 1st.

9th row K1, P8, *K1, ytf, K1, ytf, sl 1, K1, psso, K2, sl 1, K2 tog, psso, K2, K2 tog, ytf, K1, ytf, K1, P16, rep from * ending P8, K1, instead of P16.

11th row K1, P8, *K2, ytf, K1, ytf, sl 1, K1, psso, K1, sl 1, K2 tog, psso, K1, K2 tog, ytf, K1, ytf, K2, P16, rep from * ending P8, K1, instead of P16.

13th row K1, P8, *K3, ytf, K1, ytf, sl 1, K1, psso, sl 1, K2 tog, psso, K2 tog, ytf, K1, ytf, K3, P16, rep from * ending P8, K1, instead of P16.

15th row K1, P8, *K4, ytf, sl 1, K1, psso, ytf, sl 1, K2 tog, psso, ytf, K2 tog, ytf, K4, P16, rep from * ending P8, K1, instead of P16.

16th row As 2nd.

These 16 rows form the patt and are rep throughout. Continue in patt until work measures 8in from beg, ending with a RS row.

1st dec row K7, K2 tog, *P15, sl 1, K1, psso, K12, K2 tog, rep from * ending sl 1, K1, psso, K7.

Continue in patt with 1 st less in the P panels at each side and 2 sts less in the rem P panels, until work measures 14in from beg, ending with a RS row.

2nd dec row K6, K2 tog, *P15, sl 1, K1, psso, K10, K2 tog, rep from * ending sl 1, K1, psso, K6.

Continue in patt until work measures 20in from beg, ending with a RS row.

3rd dec row K5, K2 tog, *P15, sl 1, K1, psso, K8, K2 tog, rep from * ending sl 1, K1, psso, K5.

Continue in patt until work measures 26in from beg, ending with a RS row.

4th dec row K4, K2 tog, *P15, sl 1, K1, psso, K6, K2 tog, rep from * ending sl 1, K1, psso, K4.

Continue in patt until work measures 32in from beg, ending with a RS row.

5th dec row K3, K2 tog, *P15, sl 1, K1, psso, K4, K2 tog, rep from * ending sl 1, K1, psso, K3.

Continue in patt until work measures 38in from beg, ending with a RS row.

6th dec row K2, K2 tog, *P15, sl 1, K1, psso, K2, K2 tog, rep from * ending sl 1, K1, psso, K2.

Continue in patt until work measures 44in from beg, ending with a RS row.

7th dec row K1, K2 tog, *P15, sl 1, K1, psso, K2 tog, rep from * ending sl 1, K1, psso, K1 (138 sts).

Continue in patt with 2 sts in each P panel.
Work 34 rows.

Shape armholes

Bind off 8 sts at beg of next 2 rows; then 2 sts at beg of next 4 rows.

Dec one st at beg of every row until 104 sts rem.

Continue without shaping until armholes measure 6¾in from beg, ending with a WS row.

Shape shoulders

Bind off 6 sts at beg of next 4 rows; then 5 sts at beg of next 2 rows.

Shape back neck

Next row Bind off 5 sts, patt 14 sts, bind off 32 sts, patt to end.

Complete this side first.

1st row Bind off 5 sts, patt to last 2 sts, dec one st.

2nd row Dec one st, patt to end.

3rd row Bind off 6 sts, patt to last 2 sts, dec one st.

Work 1 row.

Bind off 5 rem sts.

Attach yarn to rem sts at neck edge.

1st row Dec one st, patt to end.

2nd row Bind off 6 sts, patt to last 2 sts, dec one st.

3rd row Dec one st, patt to end.

Bind off 5 rem sts.

Left front

Using No.3 needles, cast on 119 sts.

1st row K1, P8, *K6, ytf,

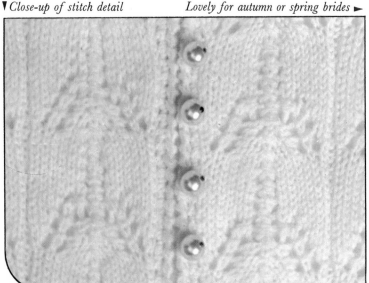

▼ *Close-up of stitch detail*

Lovely for autumn or spring brides ▶

sl 1, K2 tog, psso, ytf, K6, P16, rep from * ending P1, K1, instead of P16.

2nd and every other row K2, *P15, K16, rep from * ending K9 instead of K16. Continue in patt as set until work measures 8in from beg, ending with a RS row.

1st dec row K2, *P15, sl 1, K1, psso, K12, K2 tog, rep from * ending sl 1, K1, psso, K7. Continue in patt until work measures 14in from beg, ending with a RS row.

2nd dec row K2, * P15, sl 1, K1, psso, K10, K2 tog, rep from * ending sl 1, K1, psso, K6. Continue in patt until work measures 20in from beg, ending with a RS row.

3rd dec row K2, *P15, sl 1, K1, psso, K8, K2 tog, rep from * ending sl 1, K1, psso, K5. Continue in patt until work measures 26in from beg, ending with a RS row.

4th dec row K2, *P15, sl 1, K1, psso, K6, K2 tog, rep from * ending sl 1, K1, psso, K4. Continue in patt until work measures 32in from beg, ending with a RS row.

5th dec row K2, *P15, sl 1, K1, psso, K4, K2 tog, rep from * ending sl 1, K1, psso, K3. Continue in patt until work measures 38in from beg, ending with a RS row.

6th dec row K2, *P15, sl 1, K1, psso, K2, K2 tog, rep from * ending sl 1, K1, psso, K2. Continue in patt until work measures 44in from beg, ending with a RS row.

7th dec row K2, *P15, sl 1, K1, psso, K2 tog, rep from * ending sl 1, K1, psso, K1 (70 sts). Continue in patt with 2 sts in each P panel. Work 34 rows.

Shape armhole

At arm edge, bind off 8 sts once, then 2 sts every other row twice.

Dec one st at armhole edge on every other row until 53 sts rem.

Continue without shaping until armhole measures 5½in from beg, ending at center front edge.

1026

Shape neck

Next row Bind off 11 sts, patt to end.

Keeping armhole edge straight, dec one st at neck edge on every row 4 times, then one st on every other row twice, ending at armhole edge.

Shape shoulder

1st row Bind off 6 sts, patt to end.

2nd row Dec one st, patt to end.

3rd row Bind off 5 sts, patt to end.

4th row As 2nd.

5th row As 1st.

6th row As 2nd.

Keeping neck edge straight, bind off at neck edge 5 sts every other row twice; then 6 sts once.

Right front

Using No.3 needles, cast on 119 sts.

1st row K1, P1, *K6, ytf, sl 1, K2 tog, psso, ytf, K6, P16, rep from * ending P8, K1, instead of P16.

2nd and every other row K9, *P15, K16, rep from * ending K2 instead of K16. Continue in patt as set until work measures 8in from beg, ending with a RS row.

1st dec row K7, K2 tog, *P15, sl 1, K1, psso, K12, K2 tog, rep from * ending K2.

Complete to correspond to left front, reversing shaping, and work 1 more row before commencing armhole shaping.

Sleeves

Using No.3 needles, cast on 56 sts.

1st row K3, *P2, K4, rep from * ending K3 instead of K4.

2nd row P3, *K2, P4, rep from * ending P3, instead of P4.

These 2 rows form the patt. Continue in patt inc one st at each end of 19th and every following 10th row until there are 74 sts.

Continue without shaping until sleeve measures 12½in from beg, ending with a RS row.

Next row K2, *P1, (inc one st by picking up loop between needles and P tbl, P2) 4 times, inc one st as before, P1, K2, rep from * to end (104 sts).

Next row P2, *K6, ytf, sl 1, K2 tog, psso, ytf, K6, P2, rep from * to end.

Continue in patt as given for top of back.

Work 49 more rows.

Shape cap

Bind off 8 sts at beg of next 2 rows, then dec one st at beg of every row until 44 sts rem.

Bind off 2 sts at beg of next 4 rows; then 3 sts at beg of next 2 rows.

Bind off rem 30 sts.

Hood

Front panel

Using No.3 needles, cast on 206 sts.

1st row P2, *K6, ytf, sl 1, K2 tog, psso, ytf, K6, P2, rep from * to end.

Continue in patt as for top of back until work measures 7in from beg.

Bind off.

Back panel

Using No.3 needles, cast on 70 sts.

Work 9in patt as given for front panel.

Bind off.

Finishing

Press each piece under a damp cloth with a warm iron. Join shoulder seams.

Sew sleeves into armholes, easing fullness on each side of shoulder seam.

Join side and sleeve seams. Join bound-off and side edges of back hood panel to bound-off edge of front hood panel. Press all seams.

Hood border Thread 12 pearls onto a ball of yarn. Join in yarn and work a row of sc along face edge of hood, working one sc into each st. End with ch1 but do not turn work.

Work a row of sc back along row just worked—called crab

st—bringing a pearl to back of work at the point of each lace panel and working the st in the usual way. Cut yarn and fasten off.

Baste hood to neck edge of coat, beg 1¼in from center front edges of coat and easing in the fullness evenly.

Collar Attach yarn to right side of neck at center front edge. Work a row of firm sc right around neck edge, working through edges of both hood and coat. Turn with ch1. Work 10 more rows of sc, turning with ch1 at end of every row except last row. End last row with ch1 but do not turn work.

Work a row of crab st as given for hood border. Cut yarn and fasten off.

Front edges Attach yarn to left center front edge at top of collar and work a row of sc down left center front edge, along cast-on edges of left front, back and right front and up right center front edge to top of collar, working into every other row along center front edges and into each st along cast-on edges.

Cut yarn but do not turn. Thread 35 pearls on to ball of yarn.

Attach yarn at neck and work a row of crab st down right center front edge, working the first 12 pearls into the first and then every 5th st and the remainder into every 9th st. Continue to work in crab st along lower edges of right front, back and left front.

Cut yarn and thread rem 23 pearls onto ball of yarn. Attach yarn and continue in crab st, working pearls up left front edge to match the lower 23 pearls on right front.

Continue up left front edge, working button loops to match 12 rem pearls on right front by working ch2 and skipping one st.

Cut yarn and fasten off. Press borders lightly.

If desired, omit pearl trimming and sew on 12 small buttons, making button loops as given.

Sweet bonbon baskets and dishes

Crocheted baskets are delightful. Stiffen them with spray starch to be sure they hold their shape.

Sizes
Basket with handle
Approx. 2¼in across top.
Basket with lid
Approx. 2¼in across top.
Oval handled basket
Approx. 2½in across top.
Egg-shaped basket
Approx. 2in across top.
Large oval basket
Approx. 3¾in length of base.

Gauge
7sc and 7 rows to 1in worked on No.B crochet hook.

Materials
Coats & Clark's O.N.T. Speed Cro-Sheen 100 yd balls 1 ball each for basket with handle, oval-handled basket, egg-shaped basket and basket with lid
2 balls for large oval basket
One No. B (2.00 mm) crochet hook
Length of ½in wide ribbon for trimmings if desired

Basket with handle

Using No.B crochet hook, ch5. Join into a circle with ss.
1st round Ch2, work 7sc into circle. Join with ss to 2nd of first 2ch.
2nd round Ch2, 1sc into first sc, work 2sc into each of next 7sc. Join with ss to 2nd of first 2ch. 16sc.

3rd round Ch4, *work 1dc into next sc, ch1, rep from * to end. Join with ss to 3rd of first 4ch. 16dc.
4th round Ch2, 1sc into first ch sp, *2sc into next ch sp, rep from * to end. Join with ss to 2nd of first 2ch.
5th round Ch3, *skip 1sc, 1sc into next sc, ch3, rep from * ending with ss into ss of previous round. 16sp.
6th round Ch1, *work 2hdc into ch sp of previous round, ch1, rep from * to end. Join with ss to 1st ch.
7th round Ch2, 1hdc into same sp as ss, ch1, *work 2hdc into next ch sp, ch1, rep from * to end. Join with ss to 2nd of first 2ch.
Rep 7th round 5 times more.
13th round Work 1sc into sp immediately below ss of previous round, ch3, *work 1sc between each group of 2hdc of previous round, ch3, rep from * to end. Do not join with a ss but continue working around.
14th round *Work 1sc into ch sp, ch3, rep from * ending with ss in center of last loop of previous round. Break yarn and fasten off.

Handle
Using No.B crochet hook, ch6.

1st row Into 4th ch from hook work 1dc, 1dc into last ch. Turn.
2nd row Ch3, work 1dc into next dc, 1dc into top of turning ch. Turn.
Rep 2nd row 9 times more. Fasten off. Join handle to top of basket and trim with ribbon bow.

Basket with lid

Using No.B crochet hook, ch5. Join into a circle with a ss.
Work 1st, 2nd and 3rd rounds as given for basket with handle.
4th round 1sc into same place as ss of previous round, ch2, *work 1sc into next dc, ch2, rep from * ending with ss into first sc. 16sp.
5th round *Work 1sc into each ch sp, ch2, rep from * to end. Do not join with a ss but continue working in rounds.
Rep 5th round 4 times more, ending last round with ss in sp.
10th round Ch3, 2dc into same sp as last ss, ch2, *skip next ch sp, 3dc into next ch sp, ch2, rep from * to end. Join with a ss to 3rd of first 3ch.
11th round *Work 1sc into center dc of next 3dc group, ch2, 1sc into next ch sp, ch2, rep from * to end. Join with ss into first sc.
12th round Ss into 1st ch sp, ch3, 1dc into same ch sp, ch3, *2dc into next ch sp, ch3, rep from * to end. Join with ss into 3rd of first 3ch.
13th round Ch2, 2sc into first ch sp, *work 3sc into next ch sp, rep from * to end. Join with ss to 2nd of first 2ch. Break yarn and fasten off.

Lid
Using No.B crochet hook, ch5. Join into a circle with ss. Work first 2 rounds as given for basket with handle.
3rd round Ch4 *work 1sc into next sc, ch2, skip 1sc, rep from * to end. Join with ss to first sc. 8sp.
4th round Ss into first sp,

Left to right: basket with handle, egg-shaped basket, large oval basket dish, oval handled and lidded baskets

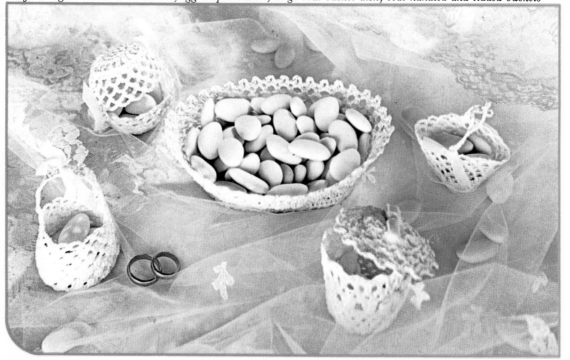

3, 2dc into same sp, ch1,
work 3dc into next ch sp,
…1, rep from * to end.
…in with ss to 3rd of first 3ch.
…h round As 11th round of
…sket.
…h round *Work 1sc into
…xt ch sp, ch3, rep from *
… end. Join with ss to first
…
…h round *Work 1sc, ch3,
…c into next ch sp, rep from
… to end. Join with ss to first
…. Break yarn and fasten off.

…nob
…ake a ribbon bow as knob.
…w knob to top of lid.

…val handled …asket

…sing No.B crochet hook,
…5. Join into a circle
…ith a ss. Work first 5 rounds
… for basket with handle.
…th round *Work 1sc into
…xt ch sp, ch2, rep from *
… end. Do not join with ss
…t continue working in
…unds.
…ep 6th round twice more,
…ding with ss in ch sp.
…th round Ch3, *1sc into
… sp, ch3, rep from * to end.
…o not join.
…0th round As 9th round.
…1th round As 9th round.
…in with ss into ch sp.
…reak yarn and fasten off.

…andles
…sing No.B crochet hook,
…20, join with ss into
…th ch from hook, ch16.
…reak yarn and fasten off.
…ork another handle in same
…ay. Twist handles tog and
…w to top of basket. Trim
…ith bows of ribbon.

…gg-shaped basket

…ork first 8 rounds as given
…r oval-handled basket.
…reak yarn and fasten off.
…ork other half of basket in
…me way. Trim sides of
…ottom half of basket with
…all bows of ribbon.

…arge oval basket

…sing No.B crochet hook,
…18.

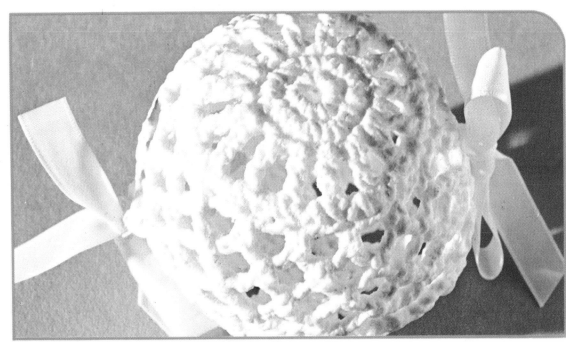

▲ *Close-up detail of the egg-shaped basket with a ribbon-trimmed lid*

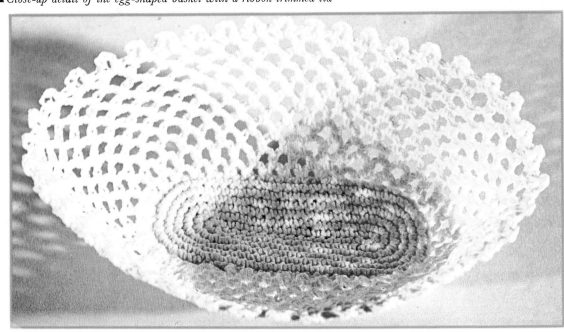

▲ *Large oval basket dish with single crochet base and picot edging*

1st round Into 2nd ch from
hook work 1sc, 1sc into each
ch to last ch, work 5sc into
last ch, do not turn work
but continue working in sc
along other side of ch to last
ch, work 5sc into last ch.
Join with ss into 2nd of first
2ch.
Continue working in sc for
5 more rounds, inc at both
ends by working 2sc into 1st
and 5th sc at each end.
7th round Work 1sc into
back loop only of each sc.
Join with ss.
8th round Work 1sc into
each sc. Join with ss.
9th round Working from
left to right, work 1sc into
each sc to form corded edge.
Join with ss. Break yarn and
fasten off.
Next round Attach yarn with
ss to front loop only of end
sc of 6th round, work 1sc
into same place as ss, ch2,
skip next sc, *1sc into next
sc, ch2, skip next sc, rep
from * to end. Join with ss
to first sc.
Next round *Work 1sc into
next ch sp, ch2, rep from *
to end. Do not join with ss

but continue working in
rounds. Rep last round three
times more.
Next round *Work 1sc
into next ch sp, ch3, rep from
* to end. Do not join with ss.
Rep last round twice more.
Next round *Work 1sc
into next ch sp, ch4, rep from
* to end. Do not join with ss.
Rep last round once more.
Join with ss to ch sp.
Next round Work 1sc, ch2,
1sc into each ch sp of
previous round.
Join with ss.
Break yarn and fasten off.

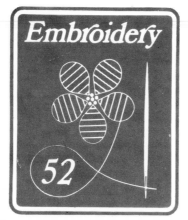

Decorating with insertions

Insertion trimmings are enjoying a new popularity. It is a delightful form of decoration involving solid areas of fabric which are joined together with lace-like stitches. This chapter deals with threads, fabrics and the methods of working.

Insertion is a method of joining two edges of fabric with decorative stitches. It looks charming on table linens and linen guest towels but it can be used to particular advantage on some kinds of clothing.

Rouleau or ribbon, alternated with insertion stitches, make a more interesting decoration for inset panels or edgings. Use either narrow or deep bands of rouleau on clothing such as on yokes or midriffs. Sleeves take on a distinctive look decorated with inset bands at intervals down their length.

Insertions are also an ideal method of adding length or letting out a garment. A deep band of rouleau set in a skirt can be worked in self fabric or fabric of a similar weight.

Fabrics

Work an insertion on a firm fabric such as fine linen, cotton, fine wool or silk. Plain colors make better backgrounds than prints or patterns.

Threads

Any medium weight embroidery thread, with the exception of 6-strand floss which is not strong enough, is suitable. All the insertions shown in this chapter are worked with D.M.C. pearl cotton No.5. If the piece of embroidery fabric is made of yarn-dyed linen or wool, threads drawn out from the fabric can be used for the insertion stitching.

Preparing the work

Make neat narrow hems on the edges to be joined or make lengths of rouleau by cutting 1 inch wide bias strips of the fabric. Fold in half lengthwise, right sides together, and make two rows of machine stitching either $\frac{1}{8}$ inch or $\frac{1}{4}$ inch from the folded edge, depending on how deep a rouleau is required. The extra fabric gives a padded, rounded effect to the rouleau. Thread the ends of the sewing thread left from the stitching into the eye of a bodkin and secure these ends with several backstitches. Slot the bodkin through the rouleau, pulling it through to the right side.

Baste the pieces of fabric, or rouleau, to heavy wrapping paper with the hemmed or rouleau edges $\frac{1}{8}$ to $\frac{1}{2}$ inch apart, depending on the finished effect desired. The further apart the hems are placed, the weaker the join will be. The two edges are then joined together with any of the following insertion stitches.

Bullion bar insertion

This is worked from right to left. Bring needle out on top edge. Cross over open space and insert needle directly below. Wrap

thread around the bar just formed one or more times depending on the width of the open space. Insert the needle in the top exactly where the thread first emerged and slide the needle through the hem to position for next bar.

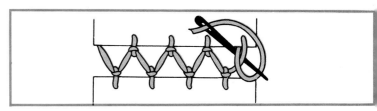

Knotted insertion

Work from left to right. Bring the thread out on the near edge and insert the needle from the front into the opposite edge. Make a loop as in buttonhole stitch, then thread the needle through as shown. Pull tight. Repeat the knot stitch on the opposite edge. Continue working a knot stitch on each edge alternately. When worked closely, this makes a firm, strong stitch.

Laced insertion

Before basting the fabric to the paper work a row of plain knotted insertion stitch along each edge separately. Baste the pieces of fabric to the paper and then lace with thread in a self or contrasting color. Work the lacing in open cretan stitch (see Embroidery chapter 13, page 250) or merely whip the edges together.

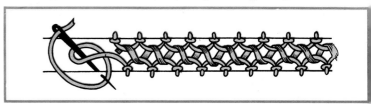

Buttonhole insertion

Working from left to right, make one or more buttonhole stitches on the top edge, then make the same number on the lower edge. The size and number of stitches can vary but should be consistent throughout one piece of work.

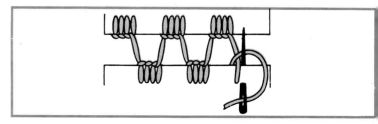

Open cretan insertion or faggoting

This is worked in the same way as cretan stitch (Embroidery 13, p. 250), picking up a small amount of fabric from alternate edges.

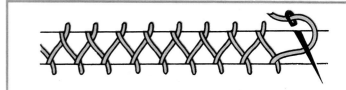

▲ *Blue linen place mat decorated with open cretan insertion worked in white*

Half cretan insertion

Work the stitches of this insertion very small and close together. A twist is formed only on one side compared with open cretan insertion in which both sides are twisted.

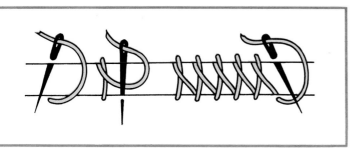

Italian buttonhole insertion

Although this stitch looks complicated, it is relatively simple and rich in effect. Begin with a loop base and buttonhole in the sequence shown. The stitches are in fact worked close together, but the diagram is spaced openly for clarity.

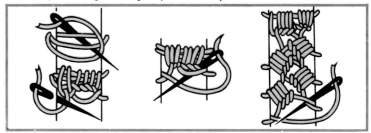

Twisted insertion

This stitch is also known as faggoting and is worked in a similar way to open cretan insertion, but as each stitch is worked the needle takes a twist over the thread of the last stitch made.

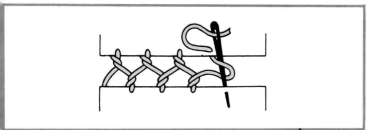

Faggot bundles insertion

The bundles are worked as shown and should be fairly close together with a firm thread, otherwise the stitch will not be rigid and will wear badly.

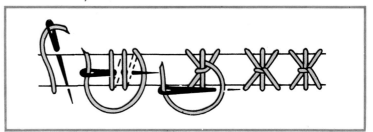

Drapery valances

A valance does not merely hide the drapery rod or drapery heading, it can help to balance the proportions of an oddly shaped window. A valance will widen a narrow window or link two small ones, give more height to a wide, shallow window or beautify a plain one. A ruffled or pleated valance does a similar job, and lends a softer line to a window. This chapter gives some variations.

Valances

A valance is a length of fabric, stiffened, cut to a chosen shape and attached to a board or rail. The board should be 4 to 6 inches deep and, whether you use a board or a rail, it should extend at least 2 inches beyond each end of the drapery rod.

Valances are usually attached to the boards with tacks but the method given in this chapter uses touch and close fastening which is easy to apply and does away with unsightly tack heads.

Valances are attached to valance rails with curtain hooks.

Suitable fabrics

Most drapery fabrics are suitable for valances, with the exception of very light or loosely woven fabrics. If your draperies are very light, then a ruffle made in the same fabric would be more effective than a stiff valance.

Measuring

Measure around the outside edge of the valance board or

window frame, from the wall at one end to the wall at the other end. This measurement is the exact length of the finished valance.

The depth of the valance and its shape are matters of per-

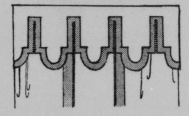

▲ **1.** *Plain and simple valance*

▲ **2.** *Valance with squared ends*

▲ **3.** *Gently curved valance*

▲ **4.** *Fringe-trimmed valance*
▼ **5.** *Scalloped valance*

sonal choice. Ideas for various shapes are given in figures 1 to 5 for you to copy. Once you have chosen the shape you want, the depth is so much a matter of proportion that it can only be finalized at the pattern making stage.

Making a pattern

You will need:
- ☐ Brown paper (Make sure that you have enough to accommodate the full length and depth for the finished valance.)
- ☐ Several large sheets of newspaper
- ☐ Pencil
- ☐ Ruler
- ☐ Scissors

Make a preliminary pattern from the newspaper.

If the newspaper sheets are not large enough to accommodate the finished size of the valance, join them together with cellophane tape. Measure off the length of the valance on the paper, then draw in the shape you have chosen for the valance to the depth required. If you have chosen a curved shape, use a suitably sized tin lid or other curved object, such as a plate, as a template for the curves.

Cut out the shape and check that the proportions are correct for the window by sticking it temporarily into position with cellophane tape.

When you are satisfied that the shape and proportions are correct, transfer the shape to the brown paper and cut it out.

Making the valance

You will need:
- ☐ The brown paper pattern
- ☐ Covering fabric (To find out how much you need, measure the length of the paper pattern and the depth at the deepest point and add 1½ inches all around.)
- ☐ Lining fabric (cotton sateen)
- ☐ Buckram for stiffening
- ☐ Bonded fiber fabric for interlining

(The previous three items are measured as for the covering fabric.)

- ☐ Matching sewing thread, basting thread
- ☐ Scissors
- ☐ Rubber cement

For attaching the valance to a valance board you will need:
- ☐ Touch and close fastening, the same length as the finished valance

Or, for attaching it to a valance rail:
- ☐ Standard curtain heading tape, the same length as the finished valance, and curtain hooks

Pin the pattern to the buckram and cut out the buckram around the edge of the pattern. Remove the pattern and cut out the bonded fiber fabric interlining in the same way.

Pin the pattern to the covering fabric and cut out the fabric leaving a 1½ inch turning allowance. Remove the pattern, pin it to the lining fabric, and cut out the lining with a ½ inch turning allowance.

Lay the interlining onto the wrong side of the covering fabric and lay the buckram onto the interlining. Baste all three together and then turn the edges of the covering fabric over the buckram, snipping into the curves and corners where necessary. Secure the covering fabric turnings to the buckram with a small amount of rubber cement. Remove the basting.

The lining

Turn under the edges of the lining for ¾ inch. Press carefully.

For attaching a valance to a valance board. Separate the two halves of the touch and close fastening and stitch the hooked length along the top edge of the turned in lining, about ¼ inch down on the right side. Machine stitch all the edges of the touch and close fastening or hand-sew with a firm hem stitch. Then lay the lining onto the valance, wrong sides facing, and hem stitch into place around the edges.

For hanging a valance from a valance rail. Stitch a length of standard curtain heading

tape along the length of the top edge of the turned in lining $\frac{1}{4}$ inch down on the right side. Finish lining the valance as before.

Hanging the valance
For a valance board. Take the remaining length of touch and close fastening (the looped side) and stick this along the valance board, flush with the top edge, with a very strong glue. When this is dry, simply press the valance into place matching the two halves of the touch and close fastening.
For a valance rail. Insert the hooks into the heading tape and hang the valance as if it were an ungathered curtain.

Ruffled valance

A ruffled or pleated valance is just like a very short curtain and is hung from a valance rail with curtain hooks. Valances can either be gathered or pleated as with curtain headings, so although you measure the valance rail in the same way as for valances, the measurement will be for the final gathered length. Decide on the depth you want the valance to be, then calculate the amount of fabric necessary as for unlined draperies (Home Sewing 5, page 494), or for pleated headings (Home Sewing 8, page 692).

For a uniform look, match the valance to the draperies in both fabric and style and use the same type of curtain heading tape for both the draperies and the valance. Figures **6** and **7** will give you ideas for styles. Make the valance as you would an unlined drapery or if you wish to line the valance use the technique for lining valances as on previous page.

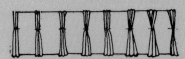

▲ **6.** *Pencil pleated valance*

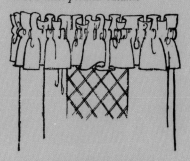

▲ **7.** *Simple gathered valance*

Needle-made lace 5

Working Aemilia-Ars lace

Aemilia-Ars lace originally came from Bologna and was famous for its delicacy and the variety of its designs. Then for a long time it was neglected until, at the end of the nineteenth century, the Aemilia-Ars Society revived this form of needlemade lace. So it is to this society that we owe the reappearance of this beautiful lace and its name.

Aemilia-Ars lace is intricate and requires great patience, but the results more than justify the effort. Unlike other forms of needlemade lace, most of which are built up as edgings or inserts onto the fabric itself, Aemilia-Ars lace is built up over its own skeleton lattice base which is prepared by a special technique.

Preparing the design

Choose a design and copy it carefully onto linen-face paper fixed to thin cardboard, or even to a piece of cardboard such as the back of a writing tablet.

Make pinholes where the lines of the motif touch the line of the surround. Using a strong thread, such as buttonhole thread, make tiny bars by threading the needle through each hole and taking it outside the outline. For the design given in this chapter, make a cross with two bars at the center where the diagonals meet.

Working the design

Starting at the bottom right-hand corner, lay the thread you have chosen for the lace (see Needle-made lace chapter 1, page 94) around the edges of the square, passing the thread under the prepared bars. Repeat once more around the outside edge, then lay one of the diagonals under the central cross, under the bar in the top left-hand corner taking in the thread of the frame, and then back to the starting point. Repeat once more to make a diagonal, three threads thick. Working down from the corner, cover the first part of the diagonal in cording (wrapping the thread around and around the core) as far as the first cross bar. Make this bar by laying a padding thread over and under the thread of the surround to the left, right, then to the left again. Work back to the diagonal covering the first half of the bar in buttonhole stitch.

Lay the third padding thread as described previously for the second half of the bar, and then work back to the center, covering the padding with buttonhole stitch.

▼ *Design trace outline with some support stitches*

▼ *Working the first corner*

▼ *Completing the second corner*

▼ *Laying base for central square*

▼ *Laying outline of star points*

▼ *Working points of the star*

Continue cording along the diagonal as far as the second bar. Work this in the same way as the first one.

Cover the diagonal in cording as far as the center. Lay part of the second diagonal from here into the bottom left-hand corner and back to the center. Then take it out to the opposite corner to lay the second half, then back to the bottom left-hand corner. Work back to the center as for the previous diagonal and cross bars.

Take the thread out to the top right-hand corner, thus laying the third thread, and work the corner in the same way as the previous two. Complete by cording back into the center again.

From the center, cord along the remaining diagonal until you reach the point where it crosses the central square. Outline the square with two padding threads and cover them in buttonhole stitch. Next lay a single base thread for the star, fixing all the points to the surrounding square, starting with the right-hand point and working counter-clockwise.

The points of the star are filled in entirely in buttonhole stitch. Work from the center outward, decreasing one stitch on each row. Work in the same counter-clockwise direction, threading through back of work to bring thread to center after each point is completed. When you have finished filling in the star, complete the fourth diagonal. Cord out from the center to the corner and work the pattern in the same way as the others.

Finishing off the motif

Finish off the framework by overcasting it. Fasten off securely, then take motif off cardboard by cutting the small thread bars.

A number of motifs can be joined together by a fine overcasting stitch.

Joining motifs together

To join Aemilia-Ars motifs together, place two right sides together, edge to edge, and neatly oversew through the threads so that the stitches are hidden at the back of the work once the seam is opened out. Or work cording over the two edges, completely covering the framework of the motifs.

Strengthen the outer edges of the completed article with buttonhole stitch or cording. If your choice is buttonhole stitch, picots can be added for further decoration.

Once the article is completed, pin the motifs out to their correct size and shape on a clean, flat surface and using rustproof pins. Cover with a damp cloth and leave until completely dry.

Joining motifs together

To insert Aemilia-Ars motifs into fabric, first lightly mark the outline of the lace onto the material either in pencil or with dressmaker's carbon paper. Make sure that the straight edges of the design follow the weave of the fabric.

Fix the motif in place on the outline and secure with small basting stitches at the center and also around the edges. Work buttonhole stitch or cording all around the edges of the motif.

Once this is completed, free the central basting stitches and then cut away the fabric within the outline using small, sharp scissors and taking care not to cut the lace. Trim close to the stitches.

▼ *The completed Aemilia-Ars lace motif enlarged to show the detail of the stitches more clearly*

▼ *Aemilia-Ars motifs used for a sleeve insert*

The softly flared sleeve in voile or chiffon with rouleau bound edge

Fine finishes for fine fabrics

This chapter gives special edge finishes for fine fabrics such as voile, chiffon, georgette and lace. These are decorative finishes which have combined with a sleeve designed especially for sheer fabrics—the softly flared sleeve illustrated here. These finishes can also be used on frills, ruffles and hem edges provided they are cut on the bias. For all the fabrics mentioned above special finishes should be applied—none are suitable for conventional hemming. Traditional couture dressmaking dictates that certain finishes should be used only on the fabrics they are best suited to. And you will notice that each finish has a certain function in completing the design. Although you will often find finishes used regardless of fabric, to the trained eye the faults stand out and can be easily detected.

In most cases the use of the machine on these fabrics should be limited to stitching seams only. When you do have to use a machine for the hem finish it is essential that you have a perfect tension.

Looking at sleeves

By changing the sleeves, you can change the style and character of a dress completely. Here are a few important points to remember when changing and adapting sleeves.

Never allow the sleeve cap to become larger than the original unless it is intended, as with a gathered cap. Check on this point by measuring the sleeve cap and comparing it with the original sleeve pattern to make sure it is not too large.

Do not lengthen or shorten the sleeve seams unless instructed to do so for making the new pattern.

Another important factor is the choice of fabric. Here, as in previous chapters, a guide is given for the correct fabric to use, but you may feel that you would like to try your own ideas. This, of course, is what dressmaking is all about.

Experienced dressmakers will know that the same style made in different fabrics, whether a dress or a blouse, requires different adjustments when fitting because the hang and fit of the garment is affected by the texture of the fabric. This also applies to sleeve shapes. So if you like a particular sleeve shape which is right for the style of the garment, but the dress fabric is wrong for the sleeves, make a compromise. Use a fabric which coordinates with the dress fabric and is suitable for the kind of sleeve shape you have chosen. If you are a beginner to dressmaking, always follow the fabric recommendations given before you experiment. That way you avoid making mistakes.

Balancing dress and sleeve

Make sure when you adapt a sleeve shape that the style of sleeve and dress complement each other and that the new sleeve shape

enhances the outfit.

Most basic dress styles look better with the addition of an attractive sleeve. But sometimes the dress itself will need a little addition at the neck, waist or hem to create a good, balanced design.

This will become obvious when you try on the dress—you may feel that something is not quite right. If so, use a scrap of fabric and try a collar, a mock tab, a belt or even a trimming around the hem line. You will see how the focus is drawn away from the sleeve and an all-over balance is achieved.

The flared short sleeve

This pattern is for the most feminine sleeve type of all—the softly flared sleeve. The best length for this sleeve is between mid-upper arm to just below the elbow, and it is usually made in a fine fabric to accentuate the delicacy of the design.

Previous chapters have given sleeve shapes adapted from the shirt sleeve pattern, while the sleeve style in this chapter is made from the straight sleeve pattern on the accessory sheet (pattern piece number 7).

You can use the short flared sleeve with any of the Creative Hand dress versions if you wish.

This sleeve is as versatile as the previous sleeve versions and the method of converting the pattern can be applied to commercial paper patterns as well.

Making the pattern

First decide on the length you want the sleeve to be and copy the straight sleeve pattern to that length. Then straighten the sleeve seams as shown (figure **1**).

Cut out the pattern and fold it lengthwise through the center to find the straight of grain and make a crease along this fold. On each side of the crease, draw five parallel lines at equal distances from each other (figure **1**). Cut the pattern on all the lines including center grain line, to within a fraction of the sleeve cap

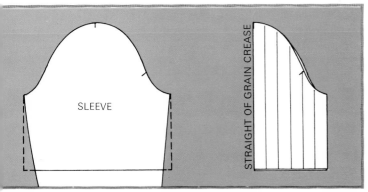

1. *Preparing the straight sleeve for spreading*

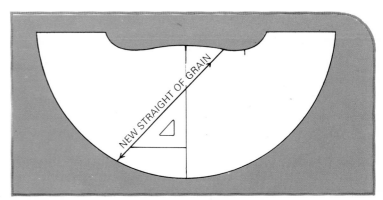

▲ **3.** *The pattern complete, with new straight of grain line*

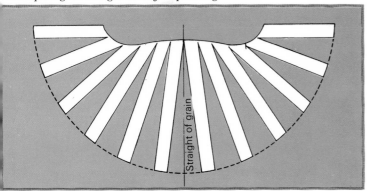

2. *Spreading the sleeve pattern*

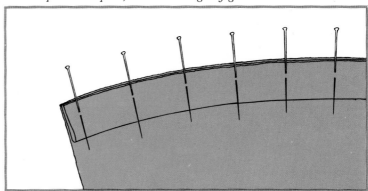

▲ **4.** *Pinning the folded bias strip to the raw edge*

On a new sheet of paper, draw a line down the center for the grain line of the pattern. Spread the pattern evenly on the paper until the sleeve seams are at right angles to the center grain line, that is on the crosswise grain (figure **2**). This line rises slightly above the sleeve cap as shown, and the hemline of the sleeve pattern should form a perfect semicircle.

Draw around the new outline, mark in all the balance marks and cut out the new pattern.

This type of sleeve looks best if cut on the bias of the fabric, so lay a 45° triangle on the straight of grain line and draw in the bias grain line (figure **3**). This bias grain line becomes the new straight of grain when cutting. When cut this way, the sleeves will fall flat over the shoulder and hang in soft folds around the hem.

Fabrics

Soft fabrics such as voiles, chiffon, lace, or georgette are the most suitable fabrics for this sleeve, but each one requires a different finish as mentioned before, and will be dealt with in turn.

Cutting and marking pattern details

Lay the new straight of grain line on the straight grain of the fabric and pin the pattern down securely.

Mark out the normal seam allowance on the sleeve cap and seams. The hem allowance is determined by the fabric and finish used, so read the instructions for your particular fabric type.

Cut out the sleeves and mark the pattern details.

Pin, baste, stitch, finish and press the sleeve seams.

If you are working in chiffon, voile or georgette, draw up the ease over the sleeve crown. Baste the sleeves into the dress and allow them to hang for at least twenty-four hours before fitting, otherwise the drop in the bias of the fabric will make the hem uneven.

Chiffon and voile

The sleeve hem in chiffon or voile should be a fine rouleau binding.

No seam allowance is required.

The double, or French, rouleau binding

Unless you are an experienced dressmaker and your speciality is working with fine fabrics, use the following method. But practice it first on scraps of fabric to get a feeling for working that particular fabric.

The rouleau must be kept narrow, no more than $\frac{1}{8}$ inch, and it must not be too tight or too loose or become too thick.

Cutting the bias strip. To try out the rouleau binding, cut a piece of the fabric with an edge curved as for the sleeves. Measure the length of the edge and cut a bias strip to this length, six times the width of a $\frac{1}{4}$ inch rouleau (that is $1\frac{1}{2}$ inches).

Ironing the bias strip. Fold the bias strip in half lengthwise and carefully press the folded edge by placing the iron on it section by section.

When finished, lift the bias strip off the ironing board and you will notice that it has become longer and slightly narrower. Lay the strip on the ironing board again and try to ease a little of the extra length back into the strip by gently pushing it with your hands.

Measure the length again and cut off any surplus.

Pinning the bias strip. Start pinning the double raw edge of the folded bias strip to the curved edge of the trial fabric, raw edges even (figure **4**).

There is a lot of stretch and movement in these fabrics, especially in chiffon, and the fabric edge as well as the rouleau edge will stretch unless you work very carefully. There are many ways to hold in or tighten the edges, such as with stay stitching, but an experienced dressmaker knows there is only one thing worse than stitching together two layers of chiffon—that is trying to stitch along the edge of one layer. In any case, you cannot control the amount of ease that stay stitching would hold in. Using tissue paper to hold the seam is another myth, as the constant movement of the pinning will tear it before you have reached the end of the seam or hem. So be prepared for some trial and error.

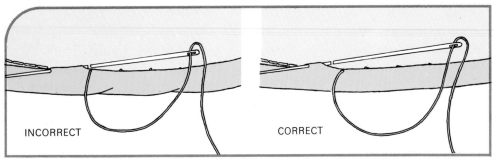

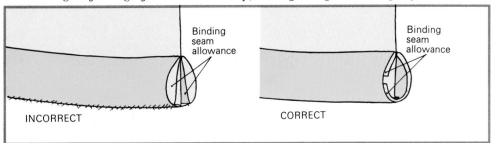

▲ 5. *Stitching the fold edge of the double bias strip, showing the right and wrong way*

▲ 6. *Extra seam allowance for a single rouleau*

▲ *The sleeve in cotton lace with whipped edge*

To pin the binding strip to the fabric edge, work on a flat surface and use very sharp pins to avoid shifting the layers of fabric as you pin them together.

Gently ease the layers of the rouleau onto the fabric edge and pin, placing the pins at right angles to the fabric edges. After pinning, baste the folded bias strip in place with fine thread and small stitches, taking ¼ inch seam allowance.

Before stitching test to see how the fabric layers have matched up. Hold the work up and see that there is no strain on it. The bias and fabric edge should hang flat, without one dragging or pulling on the other.

When you have achieved the desired result, you are ready to make the rouleau on the sleeve hem.

Preparing the bias strip for the sleeve. Measure the length of the hem on the sleeve pattern, divide by four and mark off the length of one quarter on the pattern. Then divide the sleeve hem into four equal sections; do this by folding the sleeve hem and not by measuring. Mark each quarter with pins, starting at the sleeve seam.

Cut the bias strip to the length of the hemline on the sleeve pattern plus ¼ inch seam allowance at each end. Prepare the bias strip as before but do not cut off the surplus at this point.

If you are working with voile, it is safe to trim the bias strip and join the narrow ends in the straight of the grain to form a circle to the measurement of the pattern sleeve hem.

If you are working with chiffon, you will find that the cut sleeve hem is a little more than the sleeve hemline on the pattern, so you will have to join the narrow ends of the bias strip after it has been stitched to the sleeve.

Before you trim the chiffon bias strip, divide it into the quarters of the sleeve pattern measurement. For safety, add about ½ inch of ease to each quarter, not forgetting the ¼ inch seam allowance at each end. Cut off the surplus. The ease in the bias strip may have been taken up.

Pinning the bias strip to the sleeve. Pin the bias strip to the hem edge as for the trial piece. Work from left to right, starting at the sleeve seam. Work one quarter at a time, moving on carefully and easing the layers together as you proceed along the edge.

Before basting the layers together, make sure the bias does not twist. If it does, release the pins and allow the fabric to spring back.

Stitching the bias strip. When the layers are correctly pinned together, baste the bias strip in place as before.. (With chiffon, fold the ¼ inch seam allowance into the rouleau over the sleeve seams to finish.) Stitch.

Remove the basting stitches. This must be done with great care since a caught basting stitch in such fine fabric can gather up the seamline as you try to pull the basting out. Snip the basting stitches at intervals first so that the stitches can be removed section by section.

Trim the seam allowance to about ⅛ inch so that you can fold the edge of the bias strip over it to meet the seamline easily. If your machine tension is correct, as you pick up the work you will find that there is some give in the seam. This makes it necessary for you to roll the folded bias edge over the seam allowance on a flat

surface and not fold it in your hands, o the rouleau will twist.

Completing the rouleau. The next deli cate step is hand sewing the folded edg to the seamline. In firmer fabrics you ca help control twisting by forcing stitche in the right direction, but not with fin fabrics. With these, everything you d must be well thought out and done in suc a way that pitfalls are anticipated. One o two carelessly placed stitches can ruin whole run of rouleau and you will no know about it until you have almos finished. The fault is carried on fron stitch to stitch.

So, pin the folded edge over and carefull hand sew as follows: Use the finest threa strong enough for hand-sewing and do no tighten the stitches. Let the work pas through the palm of your hand as flat a possible and do not pull it over the fore finger as this will also cause a distortio of the stitch positions. Never insert th needle into the fabric for a new stitc exactly opposite the end of the previou one but insert it a grain or two furthe on (figure **5**).

In the case of chiffon, sew the edges of th rouleau together where they meet at th sleeve seam, but make sure that you hand-sewing does not make the roulea wider here. If it should, rip the stitche Make larger stitches, which should be in serted into the very edge of each fold, an gently draw them up until you are satis fied that the width of the rouleau i correct.

The single rouleau

Here is a word of caution for dressmaker who prefer the single layer rouleau on fin

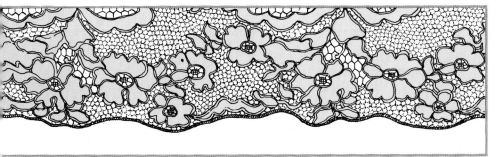

7. *Cotton lace whipped along the hem edge*

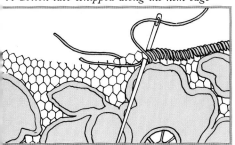

8. *Starting and ending the thread ends*

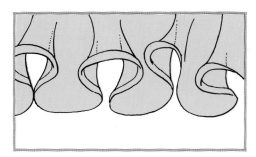

▲ **9.** *Fluted edge on georgette sleeve*

▲ *The sleeve in georgette with rolled edge*

fabrics. Unless you have plenty of seam allowance inside the rouleau, you may find that the frayed edge of the binding seam allowance works through the fine fabric of the single layer rouleau. To stop this from happening, make sure that you leave enough seam allowance to turn it under well past the rouleau foldline (figure **6**).

Laces

Cotton lace

If you are making the sleeves in soft cotton lace the hem edge should be hand-whipped and needs no seam allowance. This will give a neat, natural looking, finely rolled edge which sometimes follows the outline of the design of the lace and sometimes dips into the soft areas of net between the more solid areas of the design (figure **7**).

Use a mercerized cotton thread number 50, or a pure silk.

Work from the outside of the fabric and place the stitches so close together that they resemble a fine cord.

There is no need to fold under the edges for firmer fabrics since the stitches are placed much closer together. They are worked from right to left, like the whip stitch in Dressmaking chapter 21, page 516. Make a slightly deeper stitch when you reach areas of net or very open design. This will make the hemline dip a little and look very natural.

Start sewing without a knot in the end of the thread. Instead, lay about 1 inch of thread over the raw edge you are about to whip and catch it in as you sew. When you reach the end of the thread in the needle, cut it off leaving a short end to be caught into the stitches which follow (figure **8**)—as you will now have two threads to catch in, it is best that one is shorter than the other.

After you have worked a few stitches with the new thread, pull the two ends a little to tighten up the last stitch of the old thread and the first stitches of the new one. This way your whipped edge should look very even and any frayed edges can then be trimmed off carefully.

If this finish makes the edge curl a little, press it with an iron. If the edge is stretched so much that it cannot be pressed in, don't try to stretch the rest of the fabric to match it. You will just have to trim off the row of stitching and start again.

Unfortunately this stretching of the lace cannot be anticipated since the construction of lace varies so much. Only experience will teach you how to deal with each different type.

Nylon lace

Nylon lace is usually more difficult to work with than cotton lace. Because of this, whip stitching the edge is not as successful since the friction caused by drawing the thread through the lace when stitching will make the thread break. It is best to finish the edge with a machine zigzag.

Engage a small stitch setting and a medium zigzag width and try the stitches on the edge of a scrap of lace first. Do not pull the lace through the machine as this will stretch it and, being nylon, it will be almost impossible to ease in any fullness through pressing.

Make one row of zigzag stitches over the raw edge, trim any frayed edges and then make another row of zigzag stitches.

Georgette

To give the hem a pretty fluted edge which looks so pretty in georgette, make a fine hand-rolled hem (figure **9**).

The secret of this type of hem is to make it very hard and firm so that it pushes the fabric out and makes it curl.

There are many different types of georgette, so two methods of hand-rolling the edge are given here. Try out the first on a scrap of fabric and if it does not seem right, try out the second.

Method A

You will need a $\frac{1}{4}$ inch seam allowance. Turn under $\frac{1}{8}$ inch of seam allowance to make a neat edge and then turn under the remaining $\frac{1}{8}$ inch to complete the roll.

Hand sew in place with closely placed slip stitches to hold the roll firmly in position. Make sure that the stitches don't show on either side.

This finish should not be pressed, so be careful not to crease the hem as you work.

Method B

You will need a $\frac{3}{8}$ inch seam allowance. If method A is not successful on your fabric, turn the edge under tightly once more so that you have a double roll. This should be sufficient to give the desired result.

If the hem is still not satisfactory, then the type of georgette you are working on is probably too heavy or too loosely woven to work in this fashion, and the rouleau bound method used with voile or chiffon will be the solution.

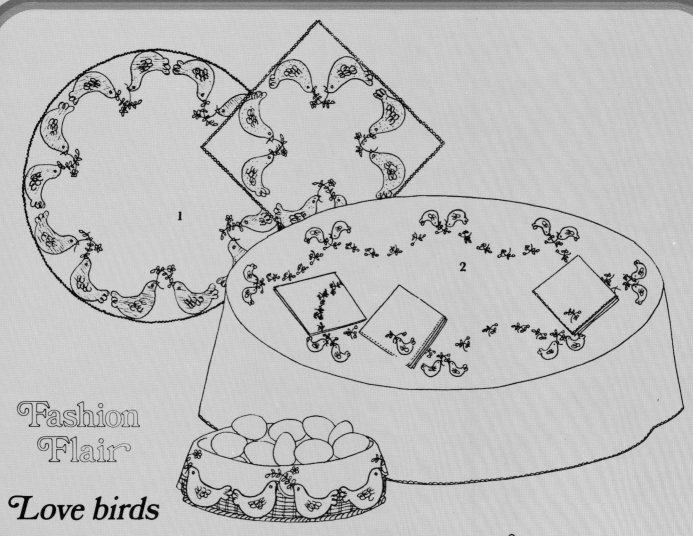

Fashion Flair

Love birds

This delightful love bird design makes a pretty decoration for all types of household linen. The simplicity of the shapes makes them ideal for appliqué, which can be further decorated with simple stitchery. Alternatively, embroider the motifs in line stitches, such as chain stitch or backstitch which can be left plain, or whipped or interlaced for added texture.

1. *Circular or square mats made of sheer organdy with appliquéd or embroidered motifs make a pretty table setting.*
2. *A circular tablecloth with napkins to match, decorated with finely embroidered love bird motifs united with leaf sprays.*

3. *A small circular cloth with a cut work edge makes a pretty lining for an egg basket.*
4. *An actual size tracing outline of the design which can be used as it is, enlarged or reduced.*
5. *Appliquéd love birds give an interesting shape in cut work on the flap of a dainty purse.*

Pattern Library

Red geometry

This needlepoint design, worked for the top of a footstool, consists of geometric patterns contained in square and rectangular shapes. The designer has made the most of the geometric nature of needlepoint stitches and formulated the design by cutting up paper shapes and rearranging them to obtain the most pleasing effect. The design is worked in crewel wool and the main stitches used are cushion stitch, rice stitch, and satin stitch. The border is worked in long legged cross-stitch and oblong cross-stitch with bars. This type of design would make a colorful wall hanging or, adapted for large mesh canvas and thicker yarns, a bright rug. The enlarged detail below shows the effect of one panel more clearly.

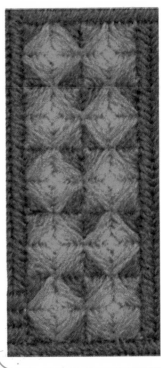

Aran poncho and matching cap

A jaunty teenage Aran poncho and cap, designed to help you to practice Aran stitches without having to cope with complicated shaping at the same time. The poncho is made in two simple, separate strips and has a neatly fitting ribbed neckband.

Size

Poncho Each piece measures 31in by 16½in, after blocking

Cap To fit 20½ to 21½in circumference measured around the head

> **Gauge**
> 9½ sts and 12 rows to 2in over stockinette stitch worked on No.7 needles.

Materials

Bear Brand, Botany or Fleisher Shamrock
8 2oz balls
One pair No.4 needles (or Canadian No. 9)
One pair No.7 needles (or Canadian No.6)
One cable needle
One No.E (3.50 mm) crochet hook

Poncho

Using No.7 needles, cast on 145 sts.
P 1 row.
Commence patt.
1st row K2, *K1 tbl, P3, K1 tbl, P2, K1 tbl, P3, K1 tbl, P11, K1 tbl, P3, K1 tbl, P2, K1 tbl, P3, K1 tbl*, P7, sl next 2 sts onto cable needle and hold at front of work, K2, K2 from cable needle—called C4F—P7**, rep from * to ** once more, then from * to * once more, K2.

2nd row K2, *P1 tbl, K3, P1 tbl, K2, P1 tbl, K3, P1 tbl, K1, (K1, P1, K1 all into next st—called 3 in 1—P3 tog) twice, 3 in 1, K1, P1 tbl, K3, P1 tbl, K2, P1 tbl, K3, P1 tbl *, K7, P4, K7**, rep from * to ** once more, then from * to * once more, K2. (151 sts).

3rd row K2, *K1 tbl, P3, K1 tbl, P2, K1 tbl, P3, K1 tbl, P13, K1 tbl, P3, K1 tbl, P2, K1 tbl, P3, K1 tbl*, P6, sl next st onto cable needle and hold at back of work, K2, P1 from cable needle—called C3B—sl next 2 sts onto cable needle and hold at front of work, P1, K2 from cable needle—called C3F—P6**, rep from * to ** once more, then from * to * once more, K2.

4th row K2, *P1 tbl, K3, P1 tbl, K2, P1 tbl, K3, P1 tbl, K1, (P3 tog, 3 in 1) twice, P3 tog, K1, P1 tbl, K3, P1 tbl, K2, P1 tbl, K3, P1 tbl*, P6, P2, K2, P2, K6**, rep from * to ** once more, then from * to * once more, K2. (145 sts).

5th row K2, *K1 tbl, P3, K1 tbl, P2, K1 tbl, P3, K1 tbl, P11, K1 tbl, P3, K1 tbl, P2, K1 tbl, P3, K1 tbl*, P5, C3B, P2, C3F, P5**, rep from * to ** once more, then from * to * once more, K2.

6th row K2, *P1 tbl, K3, P1 tbl, K2, P1 tbl, K3, P1 tbl, K1, (3 in 1, P3 tog) twice, 3 in 1, K1, P1 tbl, K3, P1 tbl, K2, P1 tbl, K3, P1 tbl*, K5, P2, K4, P2, K5**, rep from * to ** once more, then from * to * once more, K2. (151 sts).

7th row K2, *K1 tbl, P3, sl next st onto cable needle and hold at front, P1, K1 tbl from cable needle—called C2F—sl next st onto cable needle and hold at back, K1 tbl, P1 from cable needle—called C2B—P3, K1 tbl, P13, K1 tbl, P3, C2F, C2B, P3, K1 tbl*, P4, C3B, P4, C3F, P4 **, rep from * to ** once more, then from * to * once more, K2.

8th row K2, *P1 tbl, K4, (P1 tbl) twice, K4, P1 tbl, K1, (P3 tog, 3 in 1) twice, P3 tog, K1, P1 tbl, K4, (P1 tbl) twice, K4, P1 tbl*, K4, P2, K6, P2, K4**, rep from * to ** once more, then from * to * once more, K2 (145 sts).

9th row K2, *K1 tbl, P4, sl next st onto cable needle and hold at front, K1 tbl, K1 tbl from cable needle—called C2F tbl—P4, K1 tbl, P11, K1 tbl, P4, C2F tbl, P4, K1 tbl*, P3, C3B, P6, C3F, P3 **, rep from * to ** once more, then from * to * once more, K2.

10th row K2, *P1 tbl, K4, (P1 tbl) twice, K4, P1 tbl, K1, (3 in 1, P3 tog) twice, 3 in 1, K1, P1 tbl, K4, (P1 tbl) twice, K4, P1 tbl*, K3, P2, K8, P2, K3**, rep from * to ** once more, then from * to * once more, K2 (151 sts).

11th row K2, *K1 tbl, P3, C2B, C2F, P3, K1 tbl, P13, K1 tbl, P3, C2B, C2F, P3, K1 tbl *, P2, C3B, P8, C3F, P2**, rep from * to ** once more, then from * to * once more, K2.

12th row K2, *P1 tbl, K3, P1 tbl, K2, P1 tbl, K3, P1 tbl, K1, (P3 tog, 3 in 1) twice, P3 tog, K1, P1 tbl, K3, P1 tbl, K2, P1 tbl, K3, P1 tbl*, K2, P2, K10, P2, K2**, rep from * to ** once more, then from * to * once more, K2 (145 sts).

These 12 rows form patt and are rep throughout.
Keeping 2 sts in garter st each end, rep patt rows 5 times more.

Shape shoulder

Next row Patt 78 sts, *K1 tbl, P2 tog, P1, K1 tbl, P2, K1 tbl, P1, P2 tog, K1 tbl*, P2 tog, P5, C4F, P5, P2 tog,

rep from * to * once more, patt next 11 sts, rep from * to * once more, K2 (137 sts).
Continue in patt for 23 more rows, noting that there will now be one st less at each side of last 3 chain cable and V panels.
Next row Bind off 78 sts, K to end (59 sts).
Change to No.4 needles.

Neck border

1st row *K1, P1, rep from * to last st, K1.

2nd row P1, sl 1, K1, psso, *K1, P1, rep from * to last 4 sts, K1, K2 tog, P1.

3rd row K1, P1, *P1, K1, rep from * to last 3 sts, P2, K1.

4th row P1, sl 1, K1, psso, *P1, K1, rep from * to last 4 sts, P1, K2 tog, P1.

Rep last 4 rows once more, then 1st and 2nd rows once more.
Bind off in rib.
Work another piece in same way.

Finishing

Press pieces under a damp cloth with a warm iron.
Join side edge of first piece to bound-off edge of 2nd piece, and side edge of 2nd piece to bound-off edge of first piece, including neck border edges.
Fringe Cut a piece of stiff cardboard 1¾in wide and 5in long. Hold upright in left hand and knot yarn around near top. Using No.E crochet hook, put hook under loop and draw yarn through then under yarn and draw loop through again ,*wind yarn around cardboard from front to back, hook under loop at front then under yarn at back, draw through loop then draw through 2 loops on hook, rep from * for desired length, slipping loops off cardboard as it fills. When fringe fits all around poncho, break yarn but do not fasten off last st and leave a few yards of yarn for adjustment. Attach yarn at other end and work 1sc into each st of fringe, adjusting length if necessary. Top st around edges of poncho.

Cap

Using No.4 needles, cast on 91 sts.
Work 9 rows K1, P1 rib.
Next row P45 sts, P2 tog, P44 sts (90 sts).
Change to No.7 needles.
1st row (RS) P.
2nd row K1, *3 in 1, P3 tog, rep from * to last st, K1.
3rd row P.
4th row K1, *P3 tog, 3 in 1, rep from * to last st, K1.
5th row As 1st.
6th row As 2nd.
7th row *P3, K1 tbl, P2, K1 tbl, P3, rep from * to end.
8th row *K3, P1 tbl, K2, P1 tbl, K3, rep from * to end.
Rep 7th and 8th rows twice more.
13th row *P3, C2F, C2B, P3, rep from * to end.
14th row *K4, (P1 tbl) twice, K4, rep from * to end.
15th row *P4, C2F tbl, P4, rep from * to end.
16th row As 14th.
17th row *P3, C2B, C2F, P3, rep from * to end.
18th row As 8th.
Rep rows 7-18 once more.

Shape top

1st dec row P1, P2 tog, *K1 tbl, P2, K1 tbl, P2 tog, P2, P2 tog, rep from * to last 7 sts, K1 tbl, P2, K1 tbl, P2 tog, P1 (72 sts).
Work 3 rows rib tbl as now established, without shaping.
2nd dec row P2 tog, *rib 4, (P2 tog) twice, rep from * to last 6 sts, rib 4, P2 tog (54 sts).
Work 3 rows rib tbl.
3rd dec row P1, *K1 tbl, P2 tog, rep from * to last 2 sts, K1 tbl, P1 (37 sts).
Work 2 rows rib tbl.
4th dec row P1, *P2 tog, rep from * to end (19 sts).
Thread yarn through rem sts, draw up and fasten off.

Finishing

Press lightly under a damp cloth with a warm iron.
Join as shown. Make a tassel or pompon and sew to top.

◄ *Poncho featuring a simple Aran stitches pattern*

1043

Crocheted pullover with a ribbed look

Basic Wardrobe Crochet

The ribbed effect of this classic pullover is achieved by working from side edge to side edge on the body and sleeves. Collar, cuffs and edges are knitted in rib.

Sizes

Directions are for 34in bust. The figures in brackets [] refer to the 36, 38 and 40in sizes respectively.

Length to shoulder including lower ribbing, 22[22½:23:23½] in.

Sleeve seam including cuff, 17½in.

Gauge
15 sts and 18 rows over patt to 4 sq in worked on No.G crochet hook.

Materials

Sports yarn (2oz skeins) 7[7:8:8] skeins
One No. G (4.50 mm) crochet hook
One pair No.3 needles (or Canadian No. 10)

Back

Beg at side edge.
Using No.G crochet hook, ch56.

1st row Into 2nd ch from hook work 1sc, *1sc into next ch, rep from * to end. Turn.

2nd row Ch2, *1sc into next sc working into back loop only, rep from * to end. Turn. The 2nd row forms patt and is rep throughout.

Work 2[2:2:4] rows in patt. Continue in patt, inc one st at end of next row.

Work 1 row.

Shape armhole

Next row Ch20[22:24:26]. Work in patt along ch and across rem sts. 77[79:81:83] sts.

Continue in patt, inc one st at shoulder edge on 6th[8th: 8th:8th] row and every following 6th row, counting from armhole, until there are 80[82:84:86] sts.

Work 13[13:15:15] rows without shaping.

This completes one half back. Work other half to correspond, dec instead of inc and ss over 20[22:24:26] sts for armhole. Finish off.

Front

Work as given for back.

Sleeves

Beg at side edge.
Using No.G crochet hook, ch10.

1st row 1ss into each ch to end. Turn.

2nd row Ch2, *1sc into next st working into back loop only, rep from * to end. Turn.

3rd row Ch10, 1ss into each ch, work 1sc into back loop only of each sc. Turn.

4th row As 2nd.

Continue in patt, inc 10 sts at beg of next and every other row in this way until 5 groups of 10 sts have been added to the first group of 10 sts; *at the same time* shape sleeve cap by inc one st at end of 5th and beg of 6th rows, at end of 7th and beg of 8th and continuing in this way until there are 78[80:82:84] sts in all.

Work 1 row.

Next row Ch18[18:18:20] for saddle top of sleeve, ss along ch and work in patt along rem sts.

Work 6 rows without shaping. This completes half the sleeve. Work other half to correspond, dec instead of inc and ss over groups of 10 sts for underarm seam.

Finishing

Press lightly.

Cuffs Using No.3 needles, with RS facing, pick up and K46[48:50:52] sts along lower edge of sleeve. Work 1½in K1, P1 rib. Bind off in rib.

Back lower ribbing Using No.3 needles, with RS facing, pick up and K110[114:118: 122] sts along lower edge of back. Work 1½in K1, P1 rib. Bind off in rib.

Front lower ribbing. Work as given for back lower ribbing. Join saddle top of sleeves along shoulder edge of left front and back and right front, leaving back seam open.

Collar Using No.3 needles, with RS facing, pick up and K108[108:116:116] sts evenly around neck.

Work 6in K1, P1 rib. Bind off in rib.

Join right back seam and collar. Sew in sleeves to armholes.

Join side and sleeve seams.

◄ *Detail of the ribbed effect*
Pullover with saddle top shoulder ►

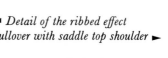

Egging you on in crochet

These cheery egg cozies are an opportunity to practice working in rounds and introducing colors. You will find it helpful to mark the first stitch of a round with contrasting thread so that you can see where it begins. Be careful when joining rounds and make sure that you do not distort the shape of the finished cozy. Finally, spray with starch.

Materials

Oddments of cotton or 3-ply yarn. One No.D (3.00 mm) crochet hook and one No.B (2.00 mm) crochet hook.

Red and white cozy

Using No.D crochet hook and red, ch5. Join into a circle with ss.

1st round. Work 12sc into circle. Join with ss to first sc.

2nd round. Ch3, *2dc into next sc, rep from * to end, 1dc into same sc as ch3. Join with ss to top of first 3ch (24dc).

3rd round. Work in sc to end, inc 1sc in every 3rd sc. Join with ss to first sc.

4th round. Work in sc to end. Join with ss to first sc.

Rep 4th round 3 times more. Break off red.

8th round. Using white, work in sc to end. Join with ss to first sc.

Rep 8th round 3 times more.

12th round. *Ch2, 1dc, 1tr, 2dtr, 1tr, 1dc, ch2, 1ss, 1sc, rep from * 3 times more. Join with ss to top of first 2ch.

13th round. Work 2sc into each space between one st and the next. Join with ss to first sc.

14th round. As 8th.

15th round. Using No.B crochet hook work *1sc, 1 ch3 picot, rep from * to end. Join with ss to first sc. Fasten off.

Using No.D crochet hook and red, make a ring by winding yarn 4 times around little finger, then cover this ring with sc. Fasten off. Attach ring to top of cozy.

Brown, green and red cozy

Using No.D crochet hook and brown, ch5. Join into a circle with ss.

Work first 2 rounds as given for red and white cozy.

3rd round. Work in sc to end, inc 1sc in every 4th sc. Join with ss to first sc (30sc). Break off brown.

4th round. Using green, work in sc to end going down every 3rd st to bottom of dc in 2nd round, draw yarn through, yoh and draw through 2 loops on hook. Join with ss to first sc.

5th round. Work in sc to end. Join with ss to first sc.

6th round. *Ch10, skip 3sc, 1sc into next sc, rep from * 6 times more. Join with ss to first of 10ch.

7th round. Keeping ch10 loops at front of work, work in sc to end, inc 1sc into every sc between 1 loop and the next. Join with ss to first sc (42sc). Break off green.

8th round. Using red work in sc to end. Join with ss to first sc.

Rep 8th round 3 times more.

12th round. 1sc, catch ch10 loop with next sc, continue in sc catching ch loop in every 6th sc. Join with ss to first sc.

Rep 8th round 6 times more.

19th round. Work in sc to end, dec one sc in every 6th sc.

Join with ss to first sc (36sc).

20th round. As 8th.

21st round. *Ch6, skip 5sc, 1sc into next sc, rep from * to end. Join with ss in first of 6ch.

22nd round. Work in sc to end, working 7sc into each ch6 loop. Join with ss to first sc. Fasten off.

Using No.B crochet hook and green work 1sc, 1hdc, 5dc, 1hdc, and 1sc to make leaf. Ch5 and work back in sc to form stem.

Fasten off. Attach leaf and stem to top of cozy.

Orange and green cozy

Using No.D crochet hook and orange, ch5. Join into a circle with ss.

Work first 4 rounds as given for red and white cozy.

Rep 4th round 4 times more. Break off orange.

9th round. Using green work in sc to end. Join with ss to first sc.

10th round. *Working into front loops of each sc work 1 picot, 1sc, rep from * to end. Join with ss to first picot.

11th round. Work in sc to end, working in back loops of sc in previous round. Join with ss to first sc. Break off green.

12th round. Using orange, as 4th round.

Rep 4th round 3 times more.

16th round. As 9th.

17th round. As 10th.

18th round. As 11th.

Rep 12th round 4 times more. Break off orange.

23rd round. Using green, *1sc, ch2, skip 1sc, 3dc, ch2, skip 1sc, rep from * to end. Join with ss to first sc.

24th round. 3sc, *1 picot, 6sc, rep from * ending with 3sc. Join with ss to first sc. Fasten off.

Using No.B crochet hook and green, ch6. Join into a circle with ss. Fasten off. Attach loop to top of cozy.

Green and white cozy

Using No.D crochet hook and green, ch5. Join into a circle with ss.

Work first 2 rounds as given for red and white cozy.

3rd round. Work in sc to end. Join with ss to first sc. Break off green.

4th round. Using white, as 3rd round.

5th round. Ch3, skip 1sc, *4dc into next sc, skip 1sc, 1dc into next sc, skip 1sc, rep from * ending with 4dc. Join with ss to top of first 3ch.

6th round. Ch3, *4dc into middle of 4dc of previous round, 1dc into 1dc, rep from * to end. Join with ss to top of first 3ch.

Rep 6th round twice more.

Break off white.

9th round. Using green, *in space between 4dc and single dc work ch placing hook between one round and the next, draw yarn through then through loop on hook, working down to last round in green then coming back in next space on other side of single dc, then work 1sc into each of 4dc on previous round, rep from * to end. Join with ss to first ch worked.

10th round. Work in sc to end. Join with ss to first sc.

11th round. 1sc, ch1, *into sc above center of 4dc work 3dc, 1 picot, 3dc, ch1, into sc between green ch work 1sc, ch1, rep from * to end.

Join with ss to first sc. Fasten off.

Using No.D crochet hook and white, ch10 and join with ss, then make another ch10 and join with ss. Work 16sc into

each circle forming a figure eight. Fasten off. Attach to top of cozy.

Green, violet and purple cozy

Using No.D crochet hook and green, ch5. Join into a circle with ss.

Work first 2 rounds as given for red and white cozy.

3rd round. Work in sc to end, inc one sc in every 6th st. Join with ss to first sc (28sc).

4th round. Work in sc to end. Join with ss to first sc. Rep 4th round 3 times more. Break off green.

8th round. Using violet, *insert hook 2 rounds down and work 2sc in same st, 1sc into next 2sc of previous round, rep from * to end.

Join with ss to first sc.

9th round. Work in sc to end, dec one sc over every other long

sc of previous round. Join with ss to first sc.

Rep 4th round 3 times more. Break off violet.

13th round. Using purple, work as 8th round.

14th round. As 9th.

Rep 4th round twice more.

17th round. *1sc, ch2, skip 1sc, work 3tr into next sc, ch2, skip 1sc, rep from * to end. Join with ss to first sc. Break off purple.

18th round. Using violet join yarn to 1sc of previous round, *work 1 picot, 2sc into ch2 loop, 1 picot and 1sc into first tr of previous round, 1 picot, skip 2nd tr, 1sc and 1 picot into 3rd tr, 2sc into ch2 loop, 1 picot, 2sc into ch2 loop, rep from * to end.

Join with ss to first picot. Fasten off.

Using No.D crochet hook and green, cover a button with sc and attach to top of cozy.

Prince and Princess Charming

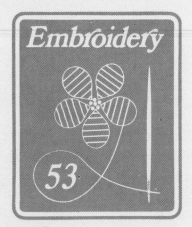

Hans Christian Andersen couldn't have dreamed up a more charming fairy-tale prince and princess than these embroidered appliqué panels. In addition to being attractive to look at when completed, they are also a delightful and satisfying project to work.

The panels illustrated each measure 17 inches by 12 inches.

You will need
For both panels
☐ ½yd cream even-weave linen for background
☐ Scraps of pink felt for faces
☐ 1 card gold lurex thread
☐ Dressmakers' carbon paper
☐ Tracing paper
☐ White glue (optional)
☐ Crewel needle size 7 or 8
☐ Hardboard 17in by 12in

For princess panel
☐ 11in by 11in blue material or felt for dress
☐ 5in by 8½in navy material for hem border
☐ 40 white sequins
☐ 40 small pearls
☐ 1 skein 6-strand floss in each of light blue, dark blue, white, deep beige, brown, red, turquoise, pink

For prince panel
☐ 10in by 12in blue material or felt for cloak
☐ 3 blue sequins
☐ 3 small pearls
☐ 1 skein 6-strand floss in each of white, light blue, brown, red, black, turquoise

To work the panels
Trace the actual size outlines and details from the following pages. Copy the half given,

fold the tracing paper in half and trace the other side to match.

Using dressmakers' carbon, transfer the outline of the figure only onto the background. Trace the outlines and embroidery details onto the pieces of fabric to be applied.

Embroider the pieces before the shapes are cut out and stitched to the background. Follow the stitch guide and apply the face first, then the dress or cloak. The navy border is applied over the dress section. Felt can be stuck down or stitched, fabric should be applied with small slip stitches. When all the embroidery and appliqué is completed, work running stitches in gold lurex thread on the background, following the fabric grain.

Special techniques
Princess panel. Use three strands of floss for all the embroidery except the bullion knots on the headdress, which are made using one strand of floss twisted three times around the needle. The couching is worked with six strands couched down with two strands. The sequins are stitched and held in place with a small pearl, worked after pressing and before mounting.

Prince panel. The French knots decorating the cloak are worked with two strands of floss, and the rest of the embroidery is worked in three strands. The double rows of couching down the front edges of the cloak and all sequins are worked in the same way as the princess panel.

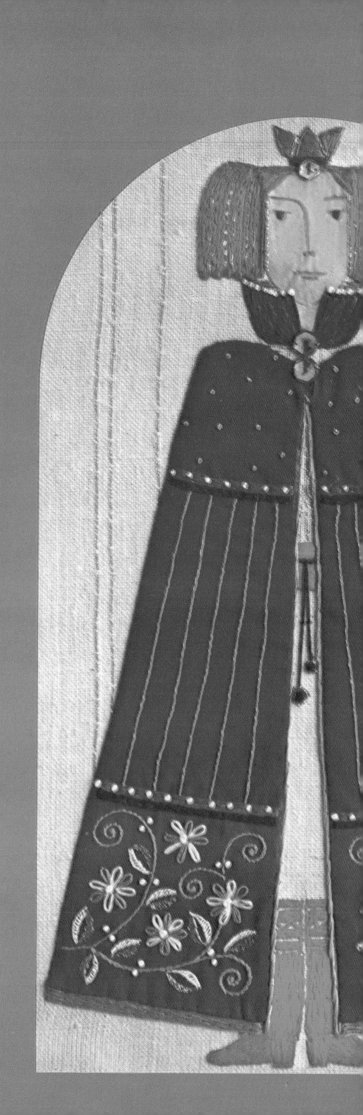

Satin stitch

French knots

Backstitch

*Full face detail of prince —
only half of the princess face
is given as this is identical
on both sides*

Satin stitch

Bullion knots

Satin stitch edged
with outline stitch

Satin stitch

Backstitch

Satin stitch

Bullion knots

Chain stitch

Backstitch

Bullion knots
surrounded with
backstitch

French knots

Bullion knots

Satin stitch

Long and short
stitch

Chain stitch

3 rows chain stitch

Sequins

Backstitch

Chain stitch

French knots

Sequins

French knots over
rows of chain stitch

Sequins

Long and short
stitch

Outline stitch

2 rows couching

Backstitch

1050

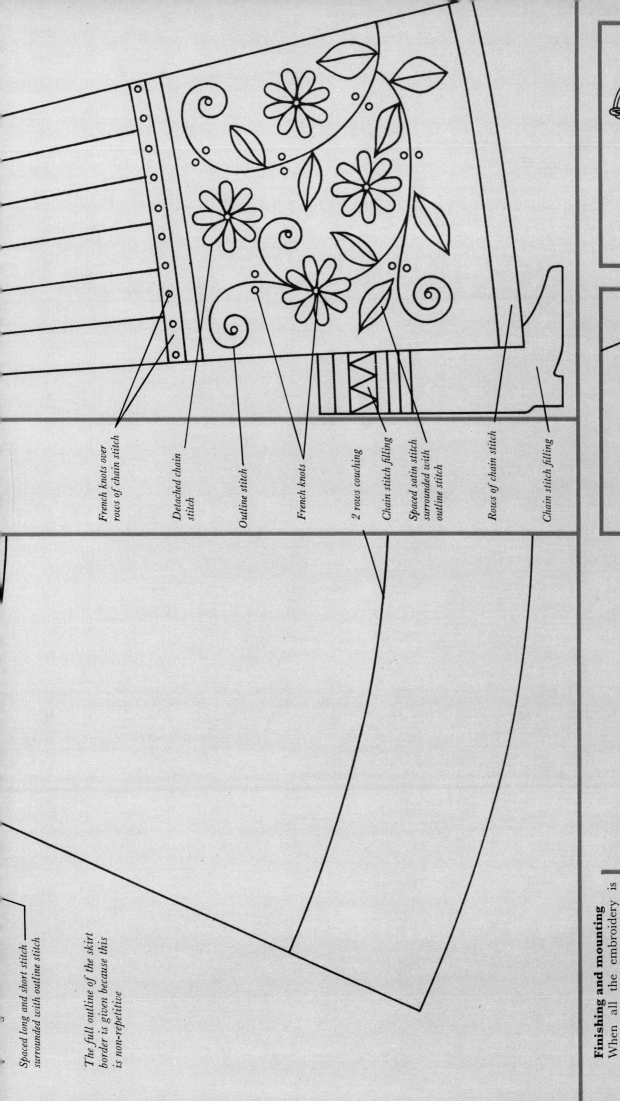

Spaced long and short stitch
surrounded with outline stitch

The full outline of the skirt
border is given because this
is non-repetitive

French knots over
rows of chain stitch

Detached chain
stitch

Outline stitch

French knots

2 rows couching

Chain stitch filling

Spaced satin stitch
surrounded with
outline stitch

Rows of chain stitch

Chain stitch filling

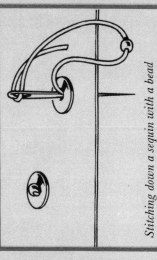

Stitching down a sequin with a bead

Work left hand the same as right

Finishing and mounting

When all the embroidery is completed and before the sequins are attached, press the work lightly on the wrong side over a well padded surface using a medium hot iron over a damp cloth. Attach sequins and mount the panels over hardboard (see Embroidery chapter 19, page 366).

▲ **Stitch guide
and tracing outline
showing half of
each panel**

Collector's Piece

Autumn flowers

This wall panel appears, at first sight, to break the basic rules of good design. The three dominating flowers are equidistantly placed immediately above one another.

The designer has, however, used various techniques, together with a limited color range, to make this an unusually effective and interesting piece of embroidery. Most of the panel has been worked by hand but some machine embroidery has been included.

The background is a natural beige-colored wool which makes an interesting contrast to the shiny, silky looking fabrics applied to it. The shapes of the leaves throughout the design are flowing and have tremendous movement. This effect is helped by the choice of embroidery stitches. The heavier, dark leaves are worked in twisted chain stitch and the paler leaves, which have a softer look, are worked in cretan stitch over applied pieces of net. Other leaf shapes are made of pieces of padded gold kid, but the stitching has been done inside the shape leaving the pointed ends free from the background. This unusual technique results in the pieces catching the light in a more interesting manner than they would stitched in the conventional way. Each of the flowers is made of layers of applied net with blocks of cretan stitch on the larger petals and sorbello stitch, twisted chain stitch and knotted chain stitch around the beaded centers. Groups of French knots and bullion knots in toning colors have been used to fill the spaces between the flowers and leaves, adding texture to the design. The glass beads added to the leaf shapes and enriching the flower centers have been placed with restraint and sensitivity.

Needle-point cover story

Snap-on covers are just the thing to up-date a favorite clutch bag, either for day or evening wear. Cover the canvas with smooth satin textures for smart occasions, rich, tweedy textures for country wear, or glittering gold or silver for evening wear. One basic bag can have a wardrobe of interchangeable covers. Two interesting stitch combinations are given in this chapter, or refer to previous Needlepoint chapters for other texture stitches which can be used.

▼ *Cushion stitch and cross-stitch combine to make an interesting pattern*

▼ *Algerian filling looks interesting when worked in a variety of colors*

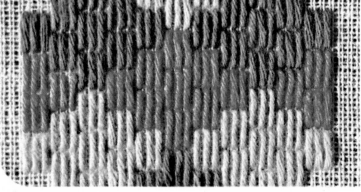

▲ *A simple clutch bag glamorized with a snap on needlepoint cover*

You will need

- ☐ A plain clutch handbag
- ☐ Sufficient canvas to cover the bag plus 2in extra all around ▮ blocking and seam allowances
- ☐ Piece of lining the same size as the canvas
- ☐ 6 large snap fasteners
- ☐ Embroidery yarn
- ☐ Tapestry needle
- ☐ Heavy paper

Making the pattern

Measure the width of the bag and then measure the length fr▮ the front flap edge, up the front of the bag, over the top and down the back edge. Draw a rectangle to these measurements on paper and cut out the pattern on the outline.

Pin the pattern onto the canvas, making sure to follow the gr▮ of the canvas. Mark the pattern outline with either basting stitc▮ or a felt-tipped pen. Find the center of the canva▮ by making ▮

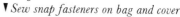

▲ *Half cushion stitch*
▼ *Sew snap fasteners on bag and cover*

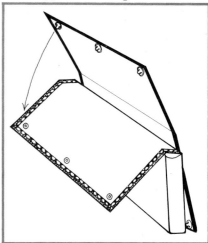

nes of basting stitches, one along the center lengthwise and the
ther across the center crosswise.
lan the design and stitches to be used.

Working the cover

Work the required area of stitching on the canvas, working out
from the center as marked by the crossed lines of basting. When
the embroidery is completed block the canvas (see Needlepoint
, page 112). Trim the canvas to within ⅝ inch of the stitching.

To make the bag

Cut the piece of lining to the same size as the trimmed canvas.
Fold the bare canvas seam allowance to the back of the work and
baste in place. Turn ⅝ inch to the wrong side of lining and press.
Place the canvas and the lining wrong sides together and baste all
round the edge. Stitch the two pieces together using a small slip
stitch. Remove basting.
Attach large snap fasteners, positioned as shown with one half of the
snap on the bag and the other half on the under side of the cover.

Cushion stitch and cross-stitch

The stitches used for the bag cover illustrated are large cushion
stitch and cross-stitch. The cushion stitch is made up of fifteen
stitches and the cross-stitch worked over two double threads of
canvas each way. To prevent too long a stitch, work on either
double thread canvas, with 15 double threads to the inch, or single
thread canvas with 18 threads to the inch. For a more decorative
finish the edge has been covered with narrow braid.

Algerian filling

This filling is made up of small blocks of satin stitch, in this case
groups of three stitches worked over four double threads of canvas. The same stitch can be worked equally well on single thread
canvas. It can either be worked entirely in one color to form a
textured background or in complementary colors to form a pattern (see also Needlepoint chapter 1, example 5, page 19).

Lounge robe for a man

Making men's clothing is often dismissed as a professional's job—and so it is for a well-tailored suit. But many of the casual clothes men wear are well within the home dressmaker's reach. A lounge or beach robe is an example of this kind of garment and as men's robes are easy to make and expensive to buy they are well worth making at home.

An ideal pattern to use is Butterick Pattern 5898, shown here in two versions—Viyella for the ¾ length robe and terry cloth in contrasting colors for the short version. The lapels and collar on the Viyella robe are made slightly narrower than those in the pattern because of the lightweight cloth. On the terry version the sleeves are made shorter—this way you can save ¼ yard of fabric.

The chapter starts off with the few fitting problems which might arise and follows with two more ways of adapting the robe pattern—to a shawl collar version, and to a judo robe with banded neckline and dropped shoulders.

Fitting the lounge robes

Baste the shoulder and side seams and adjust the armhole seam if necessary.

Bunching around the armholes

If folds appear in the Front and the Back around the armhole area as shown (figure **1**, a and b), this is due to sloping shoulders and can be corrected by pinning off the required amount at the outer edge of the shoulders, tapering to nothing at the neck, until a smooth fit is achieved (figure **1**, c).

If folds appear only at the Back or the Front, take the required amount off at the Back or the Front shoulders respectively.

Whichever shoulder has been taken up, the armhole must then be dropped by the same amount as shown (figure **1**, d).

Hanging badly

If the Front of the robe does not hang straight and swings out at the hem (figure **2**, a), it means the Front should be lifted.

Lift at the neck point by the required amount tapering to nothing at the shoulder until the Front edge hangs straight (figure **2**, b). The neckline must be lowered by the same amount as shown (figure **2**, c).

Fitting the sleeves

If you are using a thick fabric and after basting in the sleeves you find there is too much fabric in the sleeve underarm (figure **3**, a), adjust the sleeves for a smoother fit (figure **3**, b). Working on the sleeve pattern, cut 1½ inches off the sleeve seam edge on either side of the sleeve cap and taper off to nothing at the crown as shown (figure **3**, c). Then use the pattern to trim the sleeves similarly.

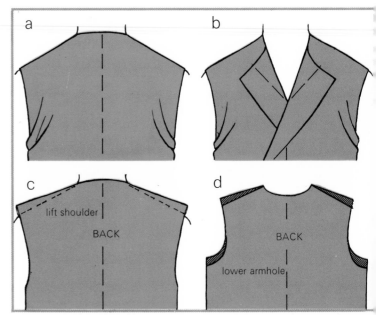

▲ **1.** *The robe bunching around the armholes: how to correct*
Butterick Pattern 5898 made in terry cloth and Viyella ▶

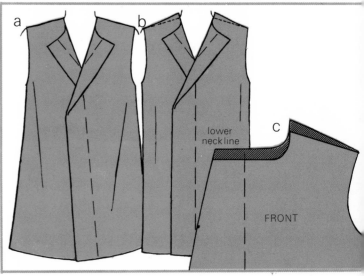

▲ **2.** *The robe hanging badly: how to correct*
▼ **3.** *Too much fabric at the underarm of the sleeves: how to correct*

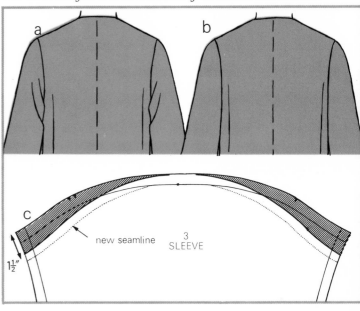

Narrower collar and lapels

When making the robe in a lightweight wool like Viyella and other fabrics of similar weight, the collar and lapels sit better if made slightly narrower than the pattern.

The pattern

To make the collar and lapels narrower, simple pattern alterations must be made to four pattern pieces—the Front (1), front facing (5), upper collar (7) and under collar (4).

Front and front facing. Starting at the inner neck edge of pattern pieces 1 and 5, take off $\frac{3}{4}$ inch tapering to nothing at the small dot as shown (figure **4**).

Upper and under collar. Alter pattern pieces 4 and 7 as shown (figure **5**), taking $\frac{3}{4}$ inch off the outer edge of each.

Making and fitting the robe

Fit the robe as shown in the fitting instructions given at the beginning of this chapter.

For making the robe, follow the appropriate instructions on the pattern intruction sheet.

▼ **4.** *Making the Front and front facing narrower*

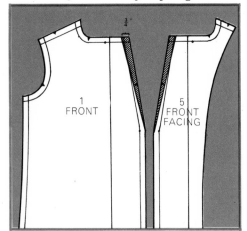

▼ **5.** *Making the upper and under collar narrower*

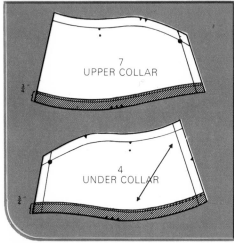

▲ *The shawl collar robe*

Shawl collar robe

Yardages

For a robe with shawl collar in one color, add $\frac{3}{8}$ yard to the yardage given on the pattern envelope. To make this robe with a contrast collar, add $\frac{1}{4}$ yard contrasting fabric and $\frac{3}{8}$ yard main fabric to the yardages given.

You will also need $\frac{1}{4}$ yard more interfacing.

The pattern

You will need the same pattern pieces as for the lapel collar versions. For the shawl collar the upper collar (7) and facing pattern pieces (5) are combined as are the Front (1) and under collar (4) pattern pieces.

Combining Front and under collar. Following figure **6**, place the under collar pattern piece on the Front pattern piece,

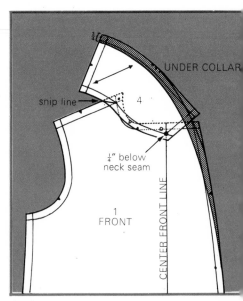

▲ **6.** *Making the New Front pattern*

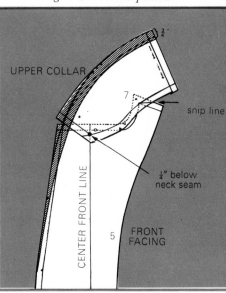

▲ **7.** *Making the new front facing pattern*

matching the small dot at the shoulder point and placing the large dot on the under collar $\frac{1}{4}$ inch down from the neck seam on the Center Front line a shown. Pin firmly in place.

Draw a line curving off the lapel point as shown by the outer solid line.

Then draw a second line $\frac{3}{4}$ inch in from the first, starting at the Center Back of the under collar and tapering to nothing at the small dot on the Front (figure **6**). Cut off the shaded area.

This pattern piece will now be referred to as the New Front.

Combining front facing and upper collar. Lay the front facing pattern piece on the Front pattern piece, matching notch 11 and the large dot on the neck seam. Trace off the Center Front line.

Using a strip of paper, add $\frac{5}{8}$ inch seam allowance to the Center Back of the upper collar.

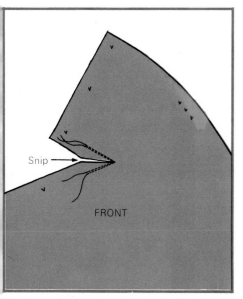

▲ **8.** *Stay stitching the snip at the neck edge*

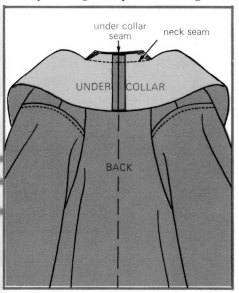

▲ **9.** *Stitching the neck seam*

Attach the upper collar and front facing pattern pieces as for the Front and under collar, and trim the collar edge similarly (figure **7**). This pattern piece will now be referred to as the new front facing.

Cutting out

Use the cutting layouts given with the pattern as a guide but use the New Front and the new front facing pattern pieces and adjust both fabric and interfacing layouts as necessary.

Making and fitting the robe

Snip the seam allowance of each New Front and new front facing to the small dot at the neck point as indicated in figures **6** and **7**. Reinforce the snips with two rows of stay stitching (figure **8**).
Fitting. Fit the robe as shown in the fitting instructions given at the beginning of this chapter.

Making. Work step 1 as for robes A, B and C on the instruction sheet.
Omit step 2 and stitch the Center Back under collar seam on the New Front and press open (figure **9**). Then stitch the neck seam as shown and press open.
Baste the interfacing to the new facing, then stitch the Center Back collar seam. Press open.
Stitch the back facing to the new front facing at the shoulder seams as shown in step **3** and press open. Then stitch together along the neck edge and press open.
Follow step **4** onward to complete the robe.

Judo robe

This robe has a banded neckline and dropped shoulders. It can be made with contrasting belt, sleeves and pocket bands.

Fabric suggestions

The judo robe can be made in any number of fabrics, but the most appropriate for this style is terry cloth with a contrasting colored band also in terry. Alternatively, the band could be in another fabric, like a strong poplin, with the tie belt and sleeve and pocket bands also in poplin.

Yardages

The yardages for both the main and contrasting fabrics are the same as those given for Robe A on the pattern envelope.
You will also need the same amount of interfacing as the original version to interface the front and back neckbands.

The pattern

For this robe you will need the same pattern pieces as for the lapel collar version except for the under collar (4), back facing (6) and upper collar (7). In addition you will need to make pattern pieces for the front, back neck and sleeve bands and to make alterations to the Front and sleeve pattern pieces. Also make a pocket band pattern.
Front. Following figure **10**, draw a line from the shoulder point to the small dot on the Front curving off the angle as shown. Cut off the shaded area.
For the dropped shoulderline, extend the shoulder seam 1½ inches, tapering to nothing at notch 3 on the armhole as shown.
Where the new lines extend beyond the original you will of course have to attach paper to the pattern to draw on the extensions.

▲ *Judo robe*

▼ **10.** *The robe front pattern*

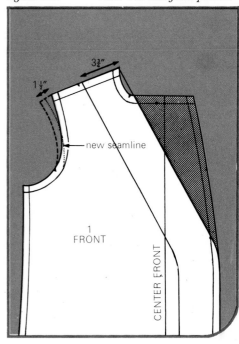

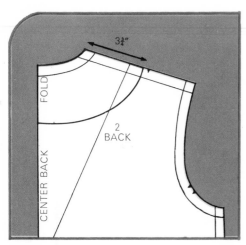

Front band. Using the New Front pattern piece, draw a second line 3¾ inches in from and parallel to the new front edge, continuing down to the hem edge (figure **10**). Trace off the front band.

Back band. Take the Back pattern piece (2) and draw a line 3¾ inches in from and parallel to the neckline (figure **11**). Trace off the back band.

Sleeve. Bend his arm and measure from the shoulder to 5 inches below the elbow. Deduct 1½ inches from this measurement to allow for the dropped shoulder and reduce the length of the sleeve pattern to this measurement (figure **12**).

Widen the sleeve hem by straightening the slanting of the sleeve seams to each side as shown. The width of the sleeve now allows for an attractive wide band.

Sleeve bands. Make a pattern for the sleeve bands 3¾ inches deep and to width of the lower edge of the sleeve.

Cutting out

Use the cutting layouts given with the pattern as a guide, but use the pattern pieces needed for the judo robe, adjusting the layout as necessary. Place the back neckband on the fold of the fabric and cut two front bands and two sleeve bands. If contrasting fabric is being used, cut the belt and the bands for the front, neck, sleeve and pocket from it.

Cut out interfacing for both front bands and for the back neckband, again cutting the back neckband on the fabric fold.

Fitting

Fit the judo robe as shown in the fitting instructions given at the beginning of this chapter.

Making the robe

Work step 1 as for robe A, B and C on the instruction sheet, except for the sleeve hem which is finished as follows.

Stitch the narrow ends of each sleeve band to form circles. Pin a sleeve band to the hem edge of each sleeve with the right side of the band facing the wrong side of the sleeve, raw edges even and sleeve seams matching. Stitch.

Turn the band to the right side and top-stitch, or under-stitch, the seam allowance to the sleeve edge to stop the sleeve hem rolling over the sleeve band (see Dress-making chapter 24, figure 5, page 476). Turn under the remaining raw edge of each band and topstitch to the sleeve close to the folded edge for a neat finish.

Omit step 2.

Turn up the hem edge of the robe and sew.

Interface the front and back neckbands, then stitch the back neckband between the front bands as shown (figure **13**).

Before attaching the neckband to the robe, stay-stitch the front and neck edges of the robe. The line from the shoulder to the point where the Front straightens out is slightly on the bias and stay-stitching will prevent any stretching which might otherwise occur.

Pin the neckband to the robe, with the right side of the band facing the wrong side of the robe, raw edges even, and with shoulder seams matching. To prevent the Front from rolling out, under-stitch along the front and neck edge.

Turn the band to the right side, turn in the seam allowance along the raw edges and topstitch close to the folded edge for a neat finish.

Follow step **5** on the instruction sheet to complete the robe and make the belt as shown.

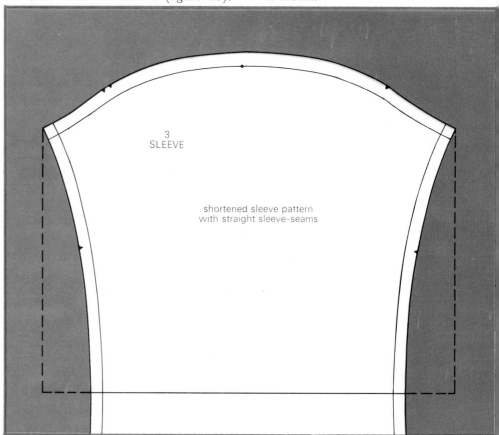

▲ **12.** *Altering the sleeve pattern*

▼ **13.** *Stitching the bands together*

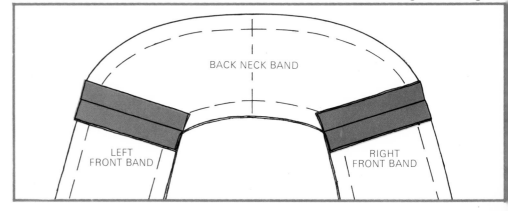

Pattern Library

Bird of Assisi

Using the close-up picture as a guide, work the outline of this Assisi design in double running or Holbein stitch, and then fill in the background with cross-stitch worked over three threads of fabric each way. Although this example has been worked in pearl cotton, 6-strand floss or matte embroidery cotton are equally suitable and should be chosen in relation to the weave of the fabric. Use the design as a border on a tablecloth or as a center motif on a small pillow.

The Fair Isle of Shetland

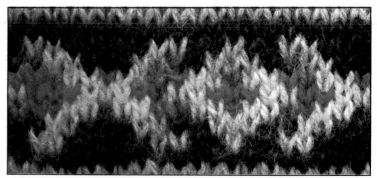

▲ *Fair Isle pattern based on a simple "O" and "X" design*

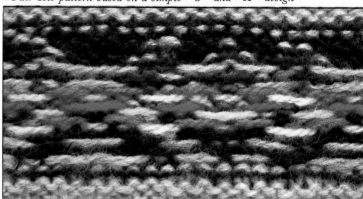

▲ *The "O" and "X" design viewed from the wrong side*
▼ *Working chart for the "O" and "X" design*

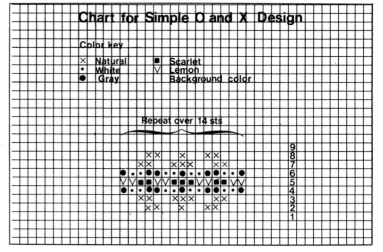

The bands of Fair Isle pattern were based on simple "O" and "X" shapes, often with the Spanish cross superimposed in the center, but were given an added subtlety by the changes of colors worked into the background in stripes, as well as the pattern itself. The softly twisted yarn was orginally "natural" in color, which could vary from white to a dark blackish brown, whatever the color of the sheep from which it came. These soft, natural tones gave the knitter a vast choice of shades to use in her pattern, but the many colors we know today were added much more recently, to cater to fashion demand.

The softness of the yarn is further enhanced by the seamlessness of the garment. Cardigans and pullovers are both knitted without seams. When the armholes are reached, the stitches are left unworked to be picked up or woven later, so that even below the arm there is no firm seam. Shoulders, too, are woven together, producing a softness and pliability of fabric which gives the garment an added charm and character.

Unlike most colored or jacquard patterns, Fair Isle designs do not have the yarns twisted on the wrong side of the fabric. Each area of color is small, and usually only two colors are used in any one row and they are carried directly from one stitch to the next to be worked in that color.

The greatest influence and change in Fair Isle work, apart from the addition of colors which the Shetlanders are so good at blending, came about during the war years of 1939-1945, when many Norwegians were stationed in Shetland. Their own colored knitting came from similar sources to those of the Shetlanders, but the motifs used were larger and more complicated. Many Fair Isle designs now incorporate these motifs most successfully. Traditionally, the patterns are handed on from mother to daughter, but where a design is written down for others to copy, the motifs are usually worked from a chart for ease of reading. Each color is marked on the chart with its own symbol. As most of the work is made by using circular or double-pointed needles to avoid seams, the right side of the work is toward the knitter who can follow the pattern visually far more quickly than attempting to read row by row instructions. Where openings are required, the work is cut later and the ends darned back in to secure them so that they do not ravel.

Simple O and X design
One of the very old, often used designs, this version repeats over 14 sts.

Flower motif
This motif is worked over 30 sts.
The colors for the motif are shown on the chart color key.
The background colors are changed on the following rows:
Rows 1 and 2   Beige.
Row 3   Light green.

Row 4	Lemon.
Rows 5-12	White.
Rows 13-15	Sand.
Rows 16-20	Lemon.
Row 21	Light green.
Rows 22-26	Lemon.
Rows 27-29	Sand.
Rows 30-37	White.
Row 38	Lemon.
Row 39	Light green.
Rows 40 & 41	Beige.

Star motif
This motif is worked over 36 sts. The colors used for the motif appear on the chart color key.
The background colors are as follows:
Rows 1-10 have beige background.
Rows 11-37 have off-white background.
Rows 38-40 have beige background.

▲ *The flower motif, worked on a changing background of rows of beige, green, lemon, white and sand.* ▼ *Working chart for the flower motif*

▲ *The star motif in tones of gray and brown on a background of beige and off-white.* ▼ *Working chart for the star motif*

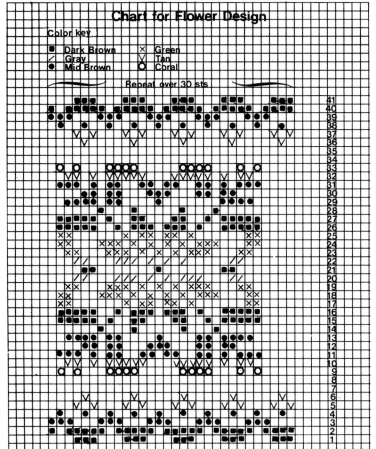

Chart for Flower Design

Color key
- ■ Dark Brown
- ╱ Gray
- ● Mid Brown
- ✕ Green
- ∨ Tan
- ○ Coral

Repeat over 30 sts

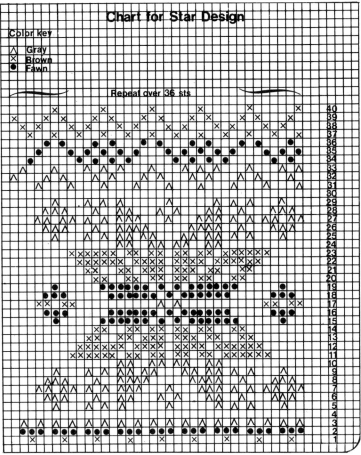

Chart for Star Design

Color key
- ∧ Gray
- ✕ Brown
- ● Fawn

Repeat over 36 sts

Trendsetting twosome in crochet

Basic Wardrobe Crochet

This lacy looking crocheted pullover, worked in a simple shell paneled stitch, is paired with a jaunty, pomponned cap worked in a cluster stitch. Although they are of dissimilar patterns, the cap and pullover, both crocheted in the same yarn, combine to make an attractive ensemble, linked by the deeper shaded edging worked on the cap, on the pullover neckline and lower edge.

Sizes

Directions are for 34in bust. The figures in brackets [] refer to the 36 and 38in sizes respectively.
Length down center back, 23½in.
Sleeve seam, 16in.

Gauge
7dc and 5 rows to 2½in worked on No.G crochet hook.

Materials

Bucilla Soufflé 1¾ oz balls
Pullover 6[6:7] balls main color A and 1[1:1] ball contrast color B
One No.G (4.50 mm) crochet hook
Cap 2 balls main color A
Small quantity contrast color B
One No. G (4.50 mm) crochet hook
One No.H (5.00 mm) crochet hook

Pullover back

Using No.G crochet hook and A, ch68[72:76].
1st row Into 2nd ch from hook work 1sc, *1sc into next

ch, rep from * to end. Turn.
2nd row (RS) Ch3, 1dc into each of next 7[9:11] sts, *skip 3 sts, work 4dc, ch1, 4dc all into next st to form 1 group, skip 3 sts, 1dc into each of next 8 sts, rep from * ending last rep with 8[10:12]dc. Turn.
3rd row Ch3, 1dc into each of next 7[9:11]dc, *ch3, 1sc into center of group, ch3, 1dc into each of next 8dc, rep from * ending last rep with 8[10:12]dc. Turn.
These 2 rows form patt and are repeated throughout.
Continue in patt until work measures 16in from beg or desired length to underarm, ending with a 3rd patt row.

Shape raglan armholes
1st row Ss over 3[4:5] sts, patt to last 3[4:5] sts. Turn.
Continue in patt, dec one dc at each end of every row until side panel dcs have been worked off and group panel sts are reached. Then dec across groups by working ½ group less on WS rows, then continue to dec 1dc at each end of every row until 1[2:3]dc, 1 group, 8dc, 1 group, 1[2:3]dc rem. Fasten off.

Pullover front

Work as given for back shaping raglan armholes in same way until 5[6:7]dc, 1 group, 8dc, 1 group, 5[6:7]dc rem.

Shape neck
Work shoulders separately on sts outside groups on either

side of central panel, working 1dc less at armhole edge as before; *at the same time* dec 1dc at neck edge on every other row until all sts have been worked off. Fasten off.

Sleeves

Using No.G crochet hook and A, ch32[32:34].
1st row As given for back.
2nd row Ch3, 1dc into each of next 4[4:5] sts, skip 3 sts, 1 group, skip 3 sts, 1dc into each of next 8 sts, skip 3 sts, 1 group, skip 3 sts, 1dc into each of next 5[5:6] sts. Turn.
3rd row Ch3, 1dc into each of next 4[4:5] sts, ch3, 1sc into group, ch3, 8dc, ch3, 1sc into group, ch3, 5[5:6]dc. Turn.
Continue in patt, inc one dc at each end of every 4th row until there are 13[13:14]dc at either side of groups.
Continue without shaping until sleeve measures 16in from beg or desired length to underarm, ending with a 3rd patt row.

Shape raglan armhole
1st row Ss over 3[4:5] sts, patt to last 3[4:5] sts. Turn.
2nd row Ss over 2 sts, patt to last 2 sts. Turn.
Rep 2nd row 3 times more.
Continue dec 1dc at each end of every row until 4[4:6]dc rem. Fasten off.

Finishing

Press lightly.
Join raglan, side and sleeve seams.
Edges Using No.G crochet hook and B, with RS of work facing, work 2 rounds sc around sleeve edges and 4 rounds sc around neck edge. Fasten off.

Cap

Using No.H crochet hook and 3 strands of A, ch3.
Join into a circle with ss into first ch.
1st round Ch2, work 5sc into circle. Join with ss into 2nd of first 2ch.
2nd round Yoh, insert hook into first st, yoh and pull up a

long st, yoh, insert hook into same st, yoh and draw up a loop, yoh and draw through all 5 loops on hook, ch1— this forms 1 cluster—work 1 cluster in same st, *2 clusters in next sc, rep from * to end. Join with ss to top of first cluster.
3rd round *1 cluster in next sp between clusters of previous row, 2 clusters in next sp, rep from * to end. Join with ss to top of first cluster.
4th round *1 cluster in each of next 2 sp, 2 clusters in next sp, rep from * to end. Join with ss to top of first cluster.
5th round *1 cluster in each of next 3 sp, 2 clusters in next sp, rep from * to end. Join with ss to top of first cluster.
6th round *1 cluster in each of next 4 sp, 2 clusters in next sp, rep from * to end. Join with ss to top of first cluster.
7th round *1 cluster in each of next 5 sp, 2 clusters in next sp, rep from * to end. Join with ss to top of first cluster.
8th round *1 cluster in next sp, rep from * to end. Join with ss to top of first cluster.
Rep 8th round 3 times more.
Change to No.G crochet hook.
12th round Ch2, *1sc into next sp, rep from * to end. Join with ss to 2nd of first 2ch.
13th round Ch2, *1sc into next sc, rep from * to end. Join with ss to 2nd of first 2ch. Break off yarn and darn in ends.

Peak

Using No.H crochet hook and 3 strands of A, ch20. Work every row sc, dec one st at beg of every row until 12sc rem. Fasten off.

Finishing

Sew peak in place. Using No.G crochet hook and 3 strands of B, work 1 row sc along all edges. Trim top with large pompon (see Crochet Know-how chapter 14, page 266).

Peaked cap and a lacy pullover ▶

The technique of Tunisian crochet

If you are interested in knitting, but haven't attempted crochet yet, you may enjoy learning the art of Tunisian crochet, a technique which combines the methods of both knitting and crochet to produce a soft, yet firm fabric. Tunisian crochet differs from both knitting and crochet in one distinctive feature—it is always worked on the right side, and is never turned. Once you have mastered the basic techniques, you will find Tunisian crochet very rewarding.

Tunisian crochet

Tunisian crochet is the complete combination of crochet and knitting and draws on the techniques of both crafts to achieve the finished fabric. Because of the way in which it is worked, Tunisian crochet produces strong, thick fabrics which are ideal for sportswear, coats, suits and heavier garments, although lighter fabrics can also be achieved. Depending on the stitch used, the finished appearance can resemble crochet or it can look surprisingly like knitting.

Using an afghan hook
The fabric is not produced with an ordinary, short crochet hook but with a special afghan crochet hook which looks exactly like a knitting needle, but with a hook at one end instead of a point. These are available in one length but, just as with crochet hooks, in a large range of sizes.

As with both knitting and crochet, the size of hook required depends on your own particular gauge, the thickness of the yarn being used and the firmness required for the final look. Experimenting with yarns and hook sizes will soon give you a very clear idea of how to achieve the desired results.

Working Tunisian crochet
Tunisian crochet takes from crochet the basic principle of beginning with a chain as explained in Crochet Know-how chapter 1, page 10. But instead of completing one stitch and then passing on to the next, it becomes like knitting and one loop from each stitch is lifted onto the hook as you work along the length of starting chain, from the right toward the left.

Although one row has now been worked, it requires a second row to complete the pattern. This is worked from left to right without turning the work around and reduces the number of loops until only one remains, when you should again have reached the right-hand edge of the work.

Once you have practiced a little, you will find the work grows quickly and is not in any way complicated.

Classic Tunisian stitch

Begin with a chain consisting of an even number of stitches.

Foundation row. Insert hook into 2nd ch from hook, put yarn around hook—called yrh—and draw one loop through ch, *insert hook into next ch, yrh and draw through one loop, rep from * to end. The number of loops on the hook should now be the same as the number of chains worked at the beginning.
2nd row. Do not turn work, yrh and draw loop through first loop on hook, *yrh and draw through 2 loops on hook, rep from * until one loop remains. This is working from left- to right-hand edge.
3rd row. Ch1, *insert hook from right to left through first upright thread of previous row, yrh and draw through one loop, rep from * into every upright thread working along the row to the left. Once again, the number of loops on the hook should be the same as the number of chains worked at the beginning.
4th row. As 2nd.
The 3rd and 4th rows are repeated for the desired length. Always finish with a 2nd row and for a neat finish work 1 row single crochet into the last row of upright threads.
Because of the way in which Tunisian crochet is worked, it has a tendency to twist sideways. This can be corrected when the finished work is pressed, but can be lessened by not working too tightly as you go along. It will be tighter if the "yrh" is not pulled adequately through the stitch so that only a tiny loop is formed and also if the yarn is held too tightly or if too fine a hook is used. When starting to work toward the right, never pull the first stitch so tightly that you flatten or pull down the height of the row.

Double Tunisian stitch

Worked over an even number of chains.
Foundation row. Yrh, insert hook into 3rd ch from hook, yrh and draw through ch, yrh and draw through 2 loops, *yrh, insert hook into next ch, yrh and draw through 2 loops, rep from * to end.
2nd row. As 2nd row of classic Tunisian stitch.
3rd row. Ch2, *yrh and insert hook from right to left into upright thread of previous row, yrh and draw through one loop, yrh and draw through 2 loops, rep from * to end.
4th row. As 2nd row of classic Tunisian stitch.
The 3rd and 4th rows are repeated for the required length.

Eyelet Tunisian stitch

Worked over an even number of chains.
Foundation row. Yrh twice, insert hook into 3rd ch from hook, yrh and draw through one loop, yrh and draw through 2 loops, *yrh twice, insert hook into next ch, yrh and draw through one loop, yrh and draw through 2 loops, rep from * to end.
2nd row. As 2nd row classic Tunisian stitch.
3rd row. Ch2, *yrh twice, insert hook into upright thread *and* slightly sloping upright thread to right of it made in previous row, yrh and draw through one loop, yrh and draw through 2 loops, rep from * to end.
4th row. As 2nd.
The 3rd and 4th rows are repeated for the desired length.

Tunisian stockinette stitch

Worked over an even number of chains.
Foundation row. As given for classic Tunisian stitch.
2nd row. As 2nd row of classic Tunisian stitch.
3rd row. Ch1, *insert hook from front to back *between* upright threads of previous row, yrh and draw through one loop, rep from * to end.
4th row. As 2nd.
The 3rd and 4th rows are repeated for the desired length. It is important to draw through a loop that is fairly loose on the hook, otherwise the work will be too tight.

▲ *Working the first row of Tunisian crochet, from right to left*

▲ *Working the second row, from left to right, without turning the work around*

▲ *Working the third row, inserting the hook into the upright thread of previous row*

▲ *Classic Tunisian stitch*

▲ *Working double Tunisian stitch*   ▼ *Tunisian stockinette stitch*

▲ *Eyelet Tunisian stitch*

▼ *Tunisian crossed stitch*

Tunisian crossed stitch

Worked over an even number of chains.

Foundation row. As given for classic Tunisian stitch.

2nd row. As 2nd row of classic Tunisian stitch.

3rd row. Ch1, *insert hook into 3rd upright thread of previous row, yrh and draw through one loop, insert hook into 2nd upright thread and draw through one loop, rep from * to end, working into 5th then 4th, 7th then 6th upright threads, etc.

4th row. As 2nd.

5th and 6th rows. As classic Tunisian stitch.

7th row. As 3rd.

8th row. As 4th.

The 5th to 8th rows are repeated for the desired length.

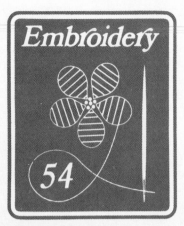

Embroidery

54

Introduction to Assisi embroidery

In the Italian town of its origin, Assisi embroidery was once used to enrich ecclesiastical linens. The unique effect is achieved by working the background in cross-stitch, leaving the design itself unworked in the basic fabric.

The designs in this chapter, typical of Assisi embroidery, are inspired by early examples which took the form of stylized birds, animals, flowers and geometric patterns taken from mosaics, wrought ironwork and carvings. The unique thing about this embroidery is that the motifs are unworked and are defined by working all around them on the outline and background only.

When to use Assisi embroidery

Assisi embroidery makes a rich decoration for household linen such as tablecloths, runners, tray or tea cart cloths, pillows and curtain hems. It also looks stunning on clothes such as on skirt or dress hems and as borders on aprons. There are several examples of motifs and borders shown in this chapter.

Suitable threads

Six-strand floss, matte embroidery cotton, pearl cotton and coton à broder are all recommended for this work. For an exotic, modern interpretation use gold lurex thread for the cross-stitch background and either black floss or lurex thread for the outlines.

Correct fabrics

This form of embroidery is worked by the counted thread and must, therefore, be worked on an even-weave fabric in either cotton or linen. Traditionally natural or cream colored fabric is used, and this type is sometimes actually called Assisi cloth.

Traditional colors

The designs are usually worked in two colors, either blue or rus

▼ *Charts for the motifs on the tea cart cloth on the facing page. The motifs have been worked the same size as the charts*

▼ *Use these motifs in a free arrangement working same size, or enlarge them by working on Binca cloth for curtains or bedspread*

▲ *A pleasing arrangement of small motifs on a tea cart cloth. Design a simple border or use one of the borders in this chapter*

▼ *A traditional Assisi animal design*

▼ *A simple geometric pattern inspired by church carvings*

for the cross-stitch background and black or some other strongly contrasting color for the double running stitch outlines.

Method of working

Two stitches only are used to form Assisi embroidery—double running or Holbein stitch (Embroidery 43, page 848) for the outlines and cross-stitch (Embroidery 12, page 228) for the background. The actual motif is left in the plain background fabric.

Both the double running stitches and the cross-stitches must be worked over the same number of threads. Work the outlines first and, once these are completed, fill in the cross-stitch background by working the cross-stitches in horizontal lines. The wrong side of the work should be perfectly even and not have long threads carried across the unworked areas of fabric.

If the outlines follow a diagonal line and it is not possible to make a complete cross-stitch the spaces can be filled in with a half cross-stitch, but it is better to arrange the design so that this is not necessary.

Finishing

A plain hem or hemstitched hem may be used but traditionally Assisi embroidery is finished with an edging of four-sided stitch (Embroidery chapter 48, page 948).

Turn the hem over once and baste. Work a row of four-sided stitch firmly over the edge of doubled fabric to give a neat, corded edge. The excess fabric is then cut away with very sharp scissors.

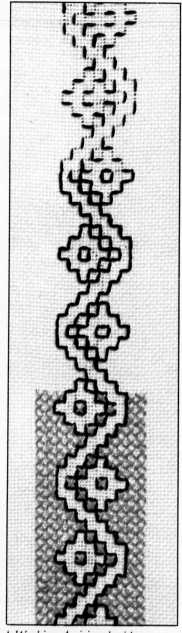

▲ *Working chart for the bird border showing one repeat*
▼ *The bird border worked on a tea cart cloth in red and black*

▲ *Working Assisi embroidery*
Bird motif enlarged for clarity ▶

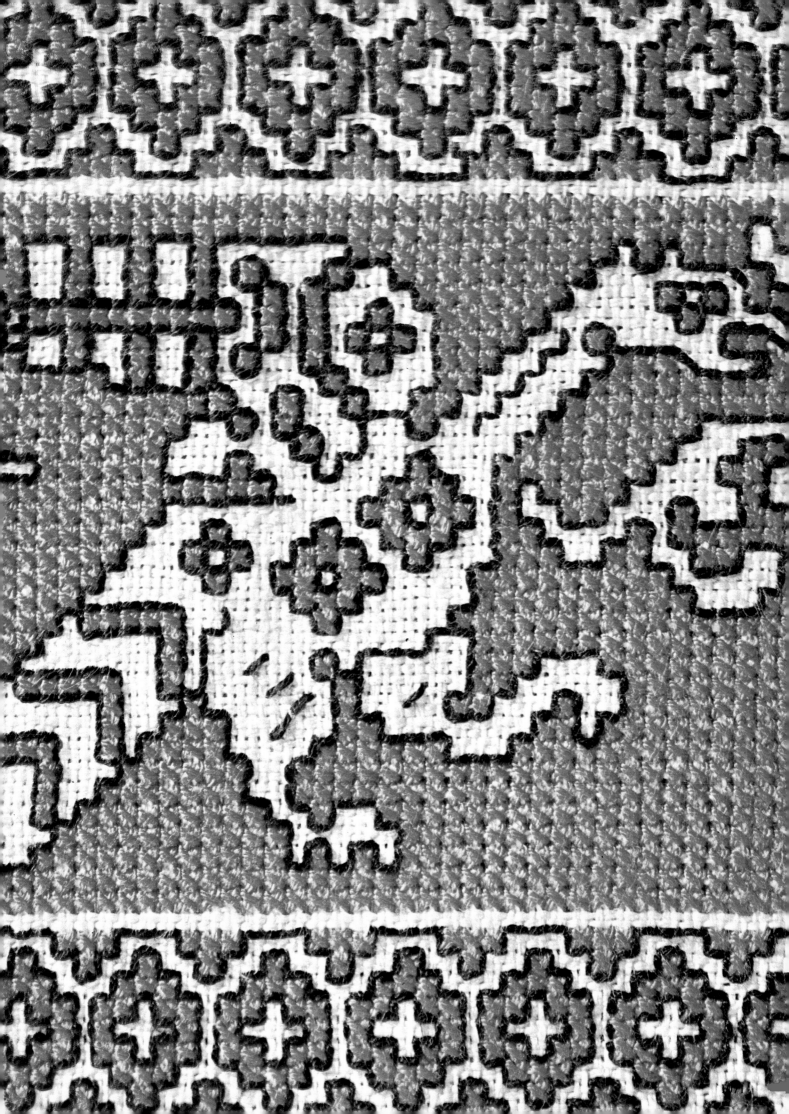

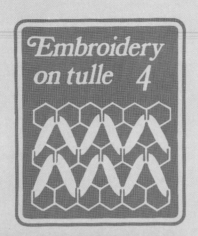

Fascinating filigree fillings

Embroidering on tulle involves a technique simple enough for you to be able to be your own designer. Therefore, the wider a repertoire of decorative filling stitches you have to draw on, the better it is. In this chapter there are seven more of these fillings to add to your range. Sometimes filling stitches can be used as individual motifs. For example, the star or spot filling given here, as well as making a very pretty filling when worked close together, could be scattered across a design, worked in between the main motifs. The spot filling is, in fact, used in just this way on the fan illustrated.

Star filling

Stars are worked by making six stitches over two or more threads of tulle, all meeting in a single mesh in the center. Secure the ends of the thread by darning them in around the center mesh on the back of the work.

Spot filling

Work a thread in running stitch around one mesh hole and then work buttonhole stitch over it to form a ring.

Grating filling

This consists of diagonal lines which cross to form a diamond pattern. Each diagonal is two rows of adjacent running stitch.

Fishbone filling

Working over three rows of meshes and from left to right, make a row of stitches which slant from left to right by inserting the needle into one hole in the first row, taking it down vertically and coming out through the mesh in the third row. Skip the next vertical row of meshes before making the next stitch in the same way.

Work a second row from right to left so that the stitches slope in the opposite direction.

◄ *The delicate filigree effect of embroidery on tulle adds to the flirtatiousness of a fan*

These two rows form the fishbone pattern.

Interlaced running stitch

The first row of running stitch is worked over as many threads as you wish. Work the second row in waves of the same dimensions, alternating and interlacing with the first row. At the end of each row make a curved line of running stitch down the side as illustrated.

Threaded stitch filling

For the first row start at the right-hand side, bringing the thread through a mesh hole from the back. Take the thread down, skipping one row of meshes, and insert the needle one hole to the right of the first mesh to form a diagonal line. Take the needle behind the mesh to the left and come out two holes along. Work a backstitch over the mesh hole skipped, bringing the needle out at the same place as last time. Take the thread back up to the first hole thus forming a diagonal line sloping to the right. Continue working back stitches over horizontal meshes linked by diagonal lines as in the illustration.

The second row is worked by passing the needle horizontally under two meshes, taking the thread down over two rows of meshes and one hole diagonally to the left, under two horizontal meshes and back up to one hole diagonally to the left. These two rows are worked alternately to form the pattern.

Ring filling

Working horizontally from right to left, begin by taking the thread over one and under one thread of tulle, and thereafter take the thread over one thread of tulle, under one over one and under one. Then working in a counter-clockwise direction, outline in running stitch the mesh hole in the row immediately below. The second row is worked three rows of meshes down, the rings worked in a clockwise direction and staggered one hole to the left of those in the row above.

Star filling

Spot filling
Grating filling

▼ *Working fishbone filling*

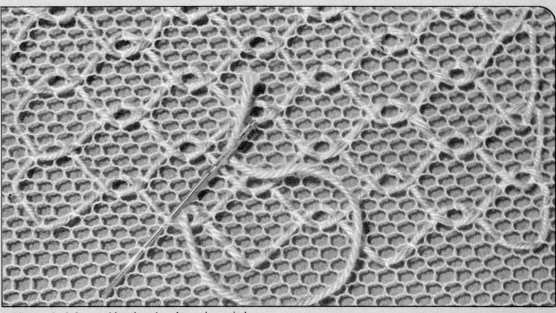

▲ *The method for working interlaced running stitch*

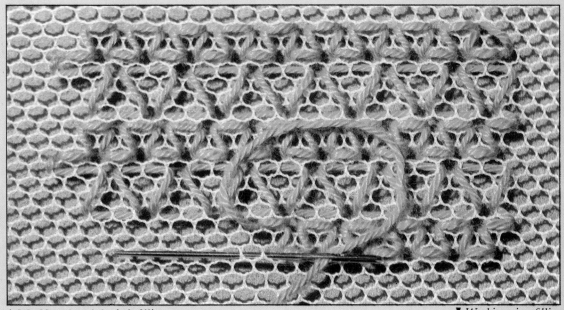

▲ *Working threaded stitch filling*   ▼ *Working ring filling*

Comfortable continental bedcovers

Introducing the duvet (pronounced doovay), the Continental way of keeping warm. These special quilts have many attributes. With a detachable cover standing in for a bedspread and top sheet, making the bed requires little effort. And because of their design, they mold around your body at night and won't slip off onto the floor. If you make one, you'll never want blankets again.

Suitable fabrics

For making the duvet case use either Dacron or Dacron and cotton mixture sheeting, and for the filling use Dacron batting. Both sheeting and batting must be 78 inches wide to give you the width you need without piecing.

For the detachable cover use Dacron, Dacron and cotton, or cotton sheeting in a 90in width.

Always use sewing threads appropriate to the fiber content of the fabric.

Bed sizes

Yardages and instructions for making both duvet and detachable cover are given for a 54in double bed size.

For other bed sizes, the fabric required is twice the bed width measurement plus 18 inches in a 78in width for the case, and a 90in width for the cover.

The amount of batting needed is equal to the bed width plus 18 inches, in a 78in width. Apart from the measurements given for the double bed size, the instructions are for all bed sizes.

Making the duvet

You will need

- ☐ 4yds 78in width sheeting
- ☐ Sheet of Dacron batting 78in by 72in
- ☐ Matching sewing thread
- ☐ Basting thread
- ☐ Extra long pins
- ☐ Tailor's chalk
- ☐ Yardstick

Cut the fabric into 2 pieces. If necessary, trim the batting to the same size (figure **1**).

Lay the fabric pieces, right sides facing, on the floor and pin them together down each long side. Baste and machine stitch plain seams $\frac{5}{8}$ inch from the edges (figure **1**).

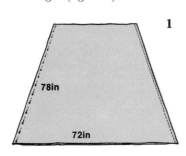

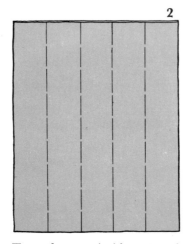

Turn the case inside out and press it. With the tailor's chalk draw 4 straight lines

from top to bottom, making 5 divisions of equal width. Trace baste these lines on each side of the case (figure **2**).

Feed the batting into the case and work it around until it lies flat and even and fills the case snugly (figure **3**).

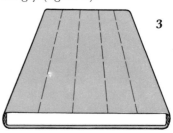

To enclose the batting, turn in the raw edges at each end of the case to a depth of $\frac{1}{2}$ inch and baste the corresponding edges together. Topstitch by machine (figure **4**).

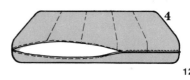

The duvet must now be stitched down the length firmly so that the batting is kept in place and will drape around your body in bed. Lay it flat on the floor, match up and pin along the trace basted lines, to include both case and filling (figure **5**). Baste along the pinned lines, through all the layers.

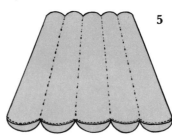

You may be able to machine stitch along the basted lines if you roll the duvet tightly under

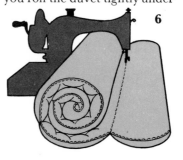

the arm of the machine and have someone help you hold it as you stitch (figure **6**).

If this is not possible, sew by hand using long, firm back stitches.

Remove all the basting threads

The detachable cover

You will need

- ☐ 4yds 90in width sheeting
- ☐ Matching sewing thread
- ☐ Basting thread, pins
- ☐ 4yds straight tape

Cut the fabric into 3 pieces (figure **7**).

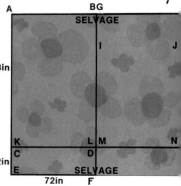

Allow $\frac{3}{4}$ inch for all seams and hems. On the back and turned in pieces machine stitch turned hems from A to B and from C to D on the wrong side of the fabric (figure **8**).

With the right sides of the fabric together, baste and machine stitch the turn-in to the front from EG to FH (figure 9).

Press both seam allowances down together and make a flat fell seam (see Home Sewing chapter 1, page 50).

9

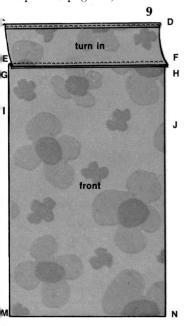

Fold down the turn-in and baste from G to I and H to J (figure 10).

10

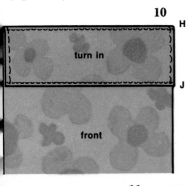

11

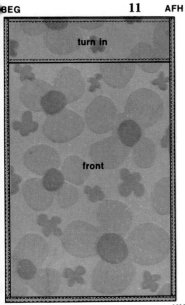

▲ *Continental quilt, or duvet, covered in patterned fabric with pillowcase and bottom sheet to match*

With right sides of the front and back together, make flat fell seams from BEG to LM, AFH to KN and LM to KN (figure 11).

Unless the duvet is tied to the duvet cover it will slip around inside. Sew 6 inch lengths of tape to the duvet as shown (figure 12).

Sew tapes to corresponding points inside the cover so that the stitching is invisible on the right side (figure 13).

12   **13**

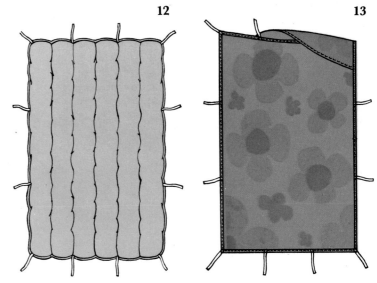

Understand your dress form

Dress forms are an invaluable aid to the home dressmaker. At those times when you need to check an inaccessible area and there is no friend at hand, a dress form can come to the rescue. Dress forms can be bought in many sizes and shapes and most women with standard measurements can find a form which will suit their shape and which needs no alteration.

But if you do have a figure problem, your clothes will need even more adjusting and a form is of even greater value. Since you cannot buy a form incorporating the problem it will require certain adjustments. You can make these yourself very easily and quickly by padding, as this chapter will show.

Of course, when choosing a form you will have to make quite sure that no part of it is larger than any of your measurements—it is one thing to pad out the form but another to make it smaller.

What you will need

Have handy some tailor's wadding (a roll of cotton will do, provided it is not too soft), some old nylon stockings, a small upholstery needle, plenty of pins and one or two old nylon slips which you won't mind cutting up. The slips are for covering the form, so if you want to give it a more decorative look buy a length of pretty printed nylon jersey instead.

If you have the problem of sloping shoulders, you will also need a pair of ready made cotton shoulder pads.

With these items you can pad the form to suit your figure—whatever your requirements.

Padding the top half of the form

Using a bodice muslin. Make yourself a bodice muslin with all the ease pinned off as shown in Dressmaking chapter 16, page 316. To find out which areas of the top half of the form need padding, pull the muslin over the form, then mark each area where the muslin does not fit properly with tailor's chalk. Remove the muslin.

Cutting the padding. Lay the wadding down flat, then cut out layers of wadding large enough to cover the whole of each marked-out area. The only area not covered this way is for sloping shoulders which are dealt with separately below.

If one layer of wadding is not sufficient to correct the shape, it will require building up with more layers.

Cut all the layers for one particular area to the same shape as the first, but reduce them in size so that you graduate the shape to follow the contours of the body (figure **1**).

Pin all wadding layers firmly in position (figure **2**).

At this stage the edges of the layers of wadding will form sharp ridges since they are the same thickness all the way through.

So pluck out the edges until each layer tapers into the shape desired.

Stitching the padding in place. Cut the nylon stockings into single layers large enough to cover each padded area.

Stretch and pin the nylon over the padding, then slip the muslin over the form again to check that it is padded correctly.

Remove the muslin and sew the nylon in place using a small upholstery needle (figure **3**). Sew to the form and avoid catching the wadding in the stitches as the thread will gather it up and distort it. You may find that you are unable to remove all the pins used for holding the wadding in place. This does not matter—the ones that remain can be left there for good, or they may eventually fall out.

Sloping shoulders. With this figure fault you will need to raise the shoulderline on each side of the neck, so use the cotton shoulder pads for this.

Slip the muslin over the form to check that the bustline of the form is in line with the bustline of the muslin.

You will find that the outer shoulder rests on the form while the inner shoulder rises above it. Pin off the excess fabric on the inner shoulder so that the shoulderline fits correctly on the form. Now the bustline of the muslin and the bustline of the form should coincide.

If the bustlines do not coincide, padding may make a difference of about 1 inch either up or down. But if the bust level varies by more than 1 inch you must disregard the bustline fitting on the form, fitting the bustline of your garments on yourself instead, and confine your fitting on the form to the shoulder, which you adjust as follows.

Cut out a small shape from the thick end of the shoulder pad so that it will fit into the neck over the shoulder seam of the form (figure **4**).

Pin the pad in position and check with the muslin that you have achieved enough lift. If not, cut out pieces of wadding to the shape of the pad but smaller, and pluck out the edges of each cut shape to flatten it. Lay these pieces under the pads to build up the inner shoulderline until the muslin fits correctly.

Cut sections from the nylon stockings to cover the pads and pin and sew in place as before.

Finishing the padded surface

If more than one area of your form is padded, it will now look slightly lumpy. To give the form the smooth appearance of a well-rounded figure, and also to give you a good and easy surface to work on, here is a quick method for making a new cover.

The cover for the form must be very close fitting, so use the muslin pattern to cut out the form cover.

Cut a bodice Back and Front from the nylon jersey, cutting both pieces on the fold and leaving seam allowances on all seamlines. The amount of seam allowance needed depends on the amount of stretch in the jersey, but this can be trimmed as necessary afterward.

Pin the Back and Front on the form. When you are satisfied that the fabric sits firmly around the form, and will not create folds when you run your hand over it, trim the seam allowance to about $\frac{1}{4}$ inch.

Overlap and pin the seam edges and hand sew them together (figure **5a**). Also hand sew the armhole, neck and waist edges firmly in place.

Padding the hipline

To complete the adjustments to the form you must, of course, also check that the hipline measurements are the same as your own. If you find that they need adjusting, work as follows.

▲ 1. *Wadding cut in graduating sizes* **2.** *Wadding pinned in place* **3.** *Covering the wadding* **4.** *Shoulder pads fitted for sloping shoulders* **5.** *Stages in covering the form; a. covering the bodice; b. covering the lower area; c. the padded form complete* **6.** *Skirt pattern adapted for form cover*

Using the basic skirt pattern from Dressmaking chapter 4, page 76, make a skirt muslin, pinning off all the ease.

Slip the skirt over the form and use tailor's chalk to mark any areas that need padding.

Cut out layers of wadding and pad the hip area as you did for the top.

Since most adjustments to the hipline will take up fairly large areas, you may find that a nylon stocking is not wide enough to cover each padded area. So pin the wadding sections very securely in place and use the nylon jersey fabric to make a solid cover.

To cut a well-fitting cover, use the basic skirt pattern for your guide. But make the following adjustments to the pattern: Straighten the side seams (figure **6**), then fold away the ease by pinning a lengthwise fold down the middle of each pattern piece as shown.

Measure the length of the form from waist to lower edge, allow a little extra length for adjustment, and cut the pattern to this measurement.

Using the adjusted pattern, cut out the nylon jersey fabric, with Center Front and Center Back on the fold of the fabric, allowing seam allowances all around.

Pin the cover to the form. Overlap the side seams and hand sew them together. The hipline cover must finish at the waistline. Handsew the waistline of the bodice and hipline covers together, having overlapped them with raw edges open (figure **5b**).

At the waist edge trim the raw edge close to the stitches then pin and baste a $\frac{1}{2}$ inch tape around the waistline (figure **5c**).

Firmly handsew the lower edge of the cover to the form so that it cannot ride up.

Pretty undies for little girls

Children's undergarments must be designed and made for practical wear. Children are not easy on their clothes, and pretty laces and fine fabrics have to withstand hard wear and frequent washing, usually in a machine. Fabric manufacturers realize this, so there is a wide choice in apparently delicate fabrics and trimming which meet the clothing standard set by a child's active life.

When you are selecting the fabric and trimming, make sure that they are of the same type of fiber, such as cotton trimming for cotton fabric. This is essential, as the wrong combination can lead to disapointing results when you wash and press the finished garments.

About finishes

Although lace and similar trimmings are very pretty, they are often very expensive. But if you make undergarments frequently, you should watch the trimmings counter of your local store. At sale times they generally sell batches of narrow lace in varying yardages which are much cheaper than when cut from a complete length. For everyday undergarments you may like to use less costly methods for the trimming, so here are some suggestions for doing this.

Frills. If you want to make fabric frills for slips, there are several economical ways to finish them.

You can stitch the hem of the frill with a pretty shell stitch, as featured in Dressmaking chapter 24, page 476, or a machine scalloped border is an attractive alternative. If you are working a shell finish, this can be repeated around the neck and armholes. You can attach the frill to the garment with a narrow lace insertion, and narrow lace trimming can be applied to the hem of the fabric frill for a very attractive finish.

Neck and armhole edges. These edges, which come into close contact with the body, must be given particular attention because they can chafe and irritate a child's skin.

So, if you know that your child's skin is very sensitive, avoid a self rouleau finish for neck and armholes and buy a length of ready-folded soft cotton bias binding and make a bias bound edge finish.

The leg edges of panties must also be kept soft so that they do not chafe or irritate. This will be discussed in the instructions which follow.

1078

Slip

The pattern

The child's basic dress pattern in Dressmaking chapter 25, page 496 is altered to make the pattern for the slip.

First copy the Front and Back pattern pieces and then adapt them as follows. Since children tend to get very hot when undergarments hang around them in folds, some of the ease should be taken from the pattern. To do this, take $\frac{1}{8}$ inch from the Center Front and Center Back and $\frac{1}{8}$ inch from each side seam. This will reduce ease by 1 inch all around (figure 1). Increase the size of the armholes by drawing in a new armhole line $\frac{1}{2}$ inch inside the pattern edge as shown. Also cut the neckline wider by drawing in a new line $\frac{5}{8}$ inch from the previous one.

Measure the length desired for the slip and shorten the pattern.

If you are using a wide trim, make sure you reduce the length accordingly, as shown in Dressmaking 21, page 416, as for the adult slips trimmed with lace.

Before you cut the pattern consider whether or not you will want to lengthen the slip later.

As a frilled hemline has no hem allowance, make two narrow rows of tucks parallel to the hemline, the folded depth of each being $\frac{3}{8}$ inch. To allow for this on the pattern, add $1\frac{1}{2}$ inches to the length. Cut out the new pattern and mark the following allowances on the pattern edges: $\frac{1}{2}$ inch on the side seams and shoulder seams; $\frac{1}{8}$ inch on the neckline and armhole edges (except for a shell stitched finish, when you will need $\frac{1}{4}$ inch); $\frac{1}{4}$ inch on the hemline; and $\frac{1}{2}$ inch on the Center Back seam.

Cutting out

Make a layout as shown in Dressmaking chapter 46, page 916 and calculate your yardage requirements.

The Center Front is placed on the fabric fold and the Center Back is cut for seaming. Also allow for rouleau binding and frills if you are cutting them from the fabric. Frills can be cut on the straight or the bias of the fabric, and should be $2\frac{1}{2}$ times the length around the hem to allow for a fully gathered frill.

Remember to add the seam and hem allowances given. Cut out the fabric.

You will also need

- ☐ Hem trimming, $2\frac{1}{2}$ times the length around the hemline
- ☐ One small button for fastening the Center Back
- ☐ Soft cotton bias binding (optional)
- ☐ Matching thread

Fitting and making the slip

Remove the pattern after cutting. It is not necessary to tailor's tack except for marking the position of the ease in the side seam.

Keep the pattern beside you and refer to it for the seam and hem allowances as you pin and baste ready for fitting.

Apart from the general hang, the most important fitting point is to make sure that the fabric clears the tender folds of skin around the underarm.

Make sure that the Center Back opening is long enough for the slip to go over the head without causing tears over a damaged hair style!

You are now ready to stitch.

Make French seams (see Dressmaking chapter 28, page 556) for the shoulder and side seams and press them toward the Front of the garment.

Stitch the Center Back seam as for ordinary seaming, as far as the end of the opening, and finish off the stitching securely.

To finish the opening, turn in the seam allowance and make a row of topstitching $\frac{1}{4}$ inch from the edges of the opening. If the Center Back has not been cut on the selvage, turn in the raw edge before topstitching to give a neat finish.

Finish the neck and armhole edges with a rouleau or bias binding.

Stitch on a button and work a hand-made loop at the top of the back opening to close it.

If you are making tucks, pin, baste and stitch them on the outside of the garment then press them down (figure 2).

Finishing the hemline

If you use a hem finish of ribbon slotted eyelet embroidery as shown here, work as follows.

Pin and baste the hem allowance to the outside of the slip and pin the ribbon slotting section over the raw edge so that the fold of the hemline meets the frill (figure 3).

Baste in place.

Pin and baste the upper edge of the ribbon slotting to the garment.

Working on the ribbon slotting section only, topstitch the trimming in place. To do this, work one row of stitches along the lower edge of the slotting catching in the folded edge of the hemline. Then work another row of stitches along the upper edge of the slotting just inside the edge (figure 4).

The ends of the trimming should be stitched together by making a French seam through the frilled section only and snipping the seam allowance in the ribbon slotting so that the ends can be turned in flat to avoid bulk (figure 4).

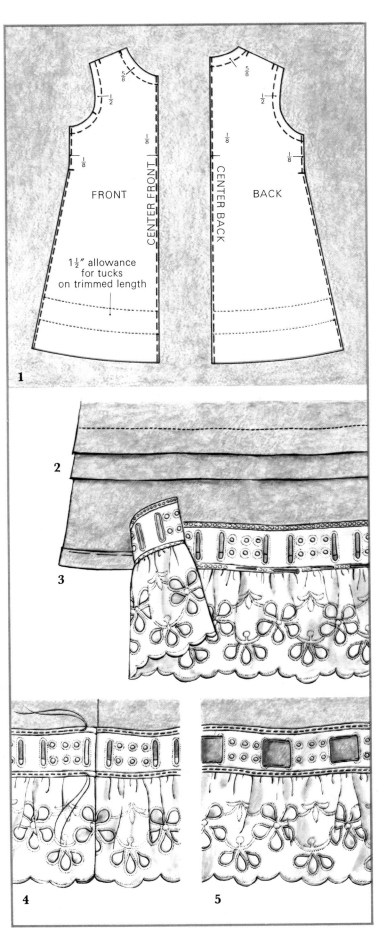

▲ **1.** *Altering the Front and Back patterns* **2.** *Tucking the hem edge*
3. *Pinning eyelet lace to hem* **4.** *Stitching eyelet lace to hem*
5. *Ribbon slotted frill*   *The slip and panties* ▶

Slotting in the ribbon

Use a brightly colored narrow ribbon to slot into the trimming (figure **5**).

Slot it in and out of the eyelets, overlap the ends, and hand sew them together. Alternatively, you can start the slotting at the Center Front leaving enough ribbon at each end to make a pretty bow. This way, if you are not quite sure if the ribbon will withstand the same washing treatment as the garment, it can easily be removed for washing.

Alternative frilled edge

If you are making a fabric frill, pin and baste the gathered edge of the frill to the hem allowance of the slip, right sides facing, raw edges even, and stitch as for an ordinary seam.

Trim the seam allowance and finish carefully. Press the seam allowance upward and then topstitch along the hemline on the outside for extra strength. If you are attaching the frill with lace insertion, make the frill less full and stitch one edge of the insertion over the raw gathered edge of the frill. Finish the seam allowance on the frill carefully, then stitch the other edge of the lace insertion to the hemline of the slip as shown for lace insertion in Dressmaking chapter 21, page 416.

Panties

The pattern

Copy the panties pattern from the graph in Dressmaking chapter 41, page 814. Mark seam allowances on the pattern edges as follows: side seams, ½ inch; crotch seam, ⅝ inch for flat-fell seaming (Dressmaking chapter 18, page 356); leg edge, ¼ inch; waist seam, ¾ inch.

Cutting out

Make a layout as shown in Dressmaking chapter 46, page 916 and calculate your yardage requirements, remembering that the panties are cut from single layers of fabric on the crosswise grain.

Remember to add the allowances as given. Cut out the fabric.

You will also need

- ☐ Eyelet embroidery edging, with a deep plain edge, to trim the leg edges (figure **6**). For each leg you will need the length of the leg hem measurement plus 3 inches for ease (for other trimming get twice the length of each leg measurement)
- ☐ Soft ¼in elastic for the legs and waist
- ☐ Matching thread

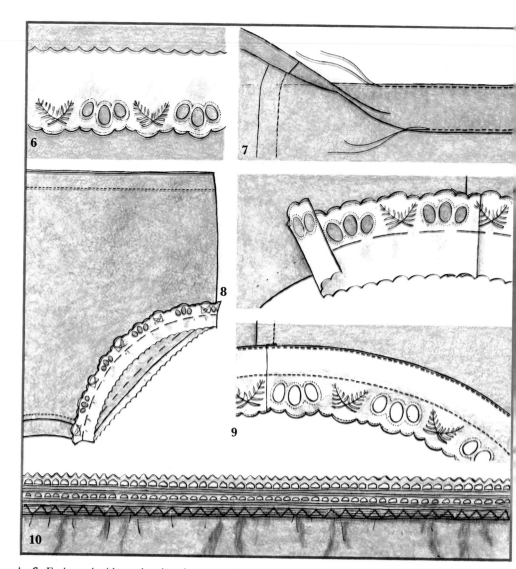

▲ **6.** *Eyelet embroidery trimming for panties* **7.** *Casing at waist of panties* **8.** *Eyelet embroidery basted to leg edge* **9.** *Leg trimming stitched in place* **10.** *Soft wide elastic stitched to waist*

Fitting and making the panties

As for the slip, it is not necessary to tailor's tack the pattern detail, but keep the pattern next to you to check on the seam allowances as you baste them. Make a flat-fell seam for the crotch seam. Then stitch the side seams with a French seam (Dressmaking chapter 28, page 556). Press the seams toward the Front.

To make a casing at the waist edge, turn under the raw edge ¼ inch, then the rest of the seam allowance, and stitch the lower fold in place (figure **7**). Also stitch the upper fold to prevent it from rolling over.

Finish the leg edge with the eyelet embroidery edging. With right sides facing, pin and baste the seamline of the leg edge close to the embroidery (figure **8**). Overlap the ends at the side seams, and ease the trimming onto the seamline so that when the leg edge is turned up the eyelet embroidery will follow the curve and not pull in the fabric.

To make the casing for the elastic, turn under the raw edge of the eyelet embroidery and topstitch the folded edge to the panties (figure **9**).

Leave a small opening in which to insert the elastic.

Plain leg finish. For a plain finish, use soft bias binding and make a casing as for the sleeve hems in Dressmaking chapter 38, figure 14, page 756.

Alternative waist finish. If you want to avoid the thickness of an elastic casing around the waistline, use the soft type of elastic which can be stitched to a raw edge (figure **10**). This is available in varying widths from ½ inch upward. When cutting the panties for this finish, take off the depth of the elastic from the waist edge and allow about ¼ inch seam allowance.

Finish the seam allowance carefully since the elastic is stitched to the open seam allowance.

Pin the elastic over the seam allowance and topstitch in place with a machine zigzag stitch.

Pattern Library

Mythical beast

This mythical creature is typical of those depicted in traditional Assisi embroidery. The outline and details of the beast are defined in double running or Holbein stitch, and the background is filled in with solid areas of cross-stitch. The whole design has been worked over four threads each way on even-weave linen using blue and yellow pearl cotton. This design would make a magnificent border on a tablecloth, along a curtain hem or at each end of a table runner. On coarser fabric, using thicker yarns, it would look good on a pillow cover.

Fair Isle afghan with crochet trim

The snowflake motif used for this afghan and pillow is a Fair Isle pattern based on a traditional Norwegian design, worked in two colors on a contrast background. The afghan is knitted in three strips which are joined together, edged with rows of crochet, and then finished off with a fringe.

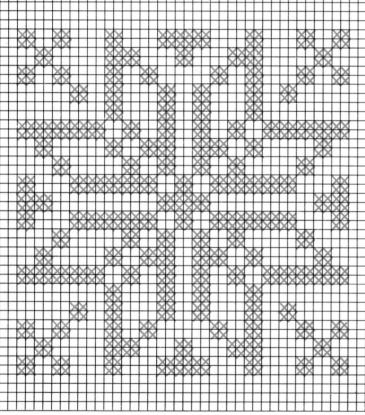

▲ *Chart for working the snowflake motif*
▼ *The snowflake motif, worked in blue on a yellow background*

Size

Afghan measures approximately 48in wide by 66in long, excluding fringe
Pillow measures approximately 15½in by 19in

> ### Gauge
> 5½ sts and 7½ rows to 1in over stockinette stitch worked on No.5 needles.

Materials

Reynolds Classique, 50 grm balls
Afghan 15 balls of main color A, yellow
4 balls of contrast color B, blue
4 balls of contrast color C, red
Pillow 2 balls of main color A, yellow
2 balls of B, blue
1 ball of C, red
One foam pad about 17in by 20in
One pair No.5 needles (or Canadian No.8)
One No.F (4.00 mm) crochet hook

Afghan

1st strip

Using No.5 needles and A, cast on 46 sts. Beg with a K row, work 4 rows st st.
5th row K4A, 2B, 2A, 2B, 4A, 2B, 4A, 6B, 4A, 2B, 4A, 2B, 2A, 2B, 4A.
6th row P4A, 2B, 2A, 2B, 4A, 2B, 4A, 6B, 4A, 2B, 4A, 2B, 2A, 2B, 4A.
7th row K6A, 2B, 6A, 4B, 4A, 2B, 4A, 4B, 6A, 2B, 6A.
8th row P6A, 2B, 6A, 4B, 4A, 2B, 4A, 4B, 6A, 2B, 6A.
9th row K4A, 2B, 2A, 2B, 4A, 2B, 2A, 2B, 6A, 2B, 2A, 2B, 4A, 2B, 2A, 2B, 4A.
10th row P4A, 2B, 2A, 2B, 4A, 2B, 2A, 2B, 6A, 2B, 2A, 2B, 4A, 2B, 2A, 2B, 4A.
11th row K10A, 2B, 2A, 2B, 4A, 2B, 2A, 2B, 4A, 2B, 2A, 2B, 10A.
12th row P10A, 2B, 2A, 2B, 4A, 2B, 2A, 2B, 4A, 2B, 2A, 2B, 10A.
13th row K14A, 2B, 4A, 2B, 2A, 2B, 4A, 2B, 14A.
14th row P14A, 2B, 4A, 2B, 2A, 2B, 4A, 2B, 14A.
15th row K4A, 10B, (2A, 2B) 4 times, 2A, 10B, 4A.
16th row P4A, 10B, (2A, 2B) 4 times, 2A, 10B, 4A.
17th row K6A, 2B, 6A, 2B, 2A, 4B, 2A, 4B, 2A, 2B, 6A, 2B, 6A.
18th row P6A, 2B, 6A, 2B, 2A, 4B, 2A, 4B, 2A, 2B, 6A, 2B, 6A.
19th row K8A, 2B, 6A, (2B, 2A) 3 times, 2B, 6A, 2B, 8A.
20th row P8A, 2B, 6A, (2B, 2A) 3 times, 2B, 6A, 2B, 8A.
21st row K4A, 2B, 4A, 10B, 2A, 2B, 2A, 10B, 4A, 2B, 4A.
22nd row P4A, 2B, 4A, 10B, 2A, 2B, 2A, 10B, 4A, 2B, 4A.
23rd row K4A, 4B, 12A, 6B, 12A, 4B, 4A.
24th row P4A, 4B, 12A, 6B, 12A, 4B, 4A.
25th and 26th rows As 21st and 22nd rows.
27th and 28th rows As 19th and 20th rows.
29th and 30th rows As 17th and 18th rows.
31st and 32nd rows As 15th and 16th rows.
33rd and 34th rows As 13th and 14th rows.
35th and 36th rows As 11th and 12th rows.
37th and 38th rows As 9th and 10th rows.
39th and 40th rows As 7th and 8th rows.
41st and 42nd rows As 5th and 6th rows.
Beg with a K row and using A only, work 4 rows st st.
These 46 rows form one motif. Rep 46 more motif rows using C in place of B.
Rep last 92 rows twice more, then first 46 rows once more. Bind off.

2nd strip

Work as given for 1st strip, reading B for C and C for B to reverse order of contrast colors.

3rd strip

Work as given for 1st strip.

Edgings

Using No.F crochet hook and A, with RS facing, work 1 round sc around all long strip edges. Work 2 rows hdc on each long side of all strips, turning with ch2.
Join long edges of strips tog, alternating color motifs.

A colorful Norwegian snowflake motif used in bright colors for a lively afghan and matching pillow

Work rows of hdc on long sides of afghan in the following sequence, turning with ch2 at the end of each row:
4 rows C, 4 rows B, 8 rows A, 4 rows C, 4 rows B, 2 rows A.
Work 4 rows of hdc in A along 2 short ends of afghan.
Press lightly on WS under a damp cloth with a warm iron.

Cut 10in long strands of A and work fringe along sides of afghan, using 3 strands for each knot.

Pillow

Work first 46 rows as given for 1st strip of afghan. Bind off. Work another piece to match.

Edging

Using No.F crochet hook and A, with RS facing, work 1 round of sc around all sides of each piece, then work 2 rounds hdc around all edges. Fasten off.
Using A work 8 rows hdc across top and lower edges of both pieces.

Work along sides of both pieces with rows of hdc in following sequence:
2 rows A, 6 rows C, 4 rows B, 2 rows A.
Fasten off.
Press lightly on WS under a damp cloth with a warm iron.
Seam 3 sides. Insert foam pad and seam 4th side.

Seven scarves in seven stitches

Whether you prefer knitting or crochet, here is a choice of seven lovely warm scarves for you to make which will brighten the coldest winter day! Each one is based on stitches and techniques explained in previous know-how chapters.

Sizes

All scarves are designed to be 96in long unless otherwise stated. The length may be altered as desired.

> ### Gauge
> 5½ sts and 7 rows to 1 in over st st worked on No.5 needles

Materials

All 2oz. balls

Chevron striped scarf
Sports Yarn
3 balls main color A, white
2 balls contrast color B, red
One pair No.5 needles
(or Canadian No.8)

Lace fringed scarf
Sports Yarn
4 balls
One pair No.5 needles
(or Canadian No.8)
One No.E (3.50 mm)
crochet hook

Woven stitch scarf
Sports Yarn
3 balls main color A
Small quantities of contrast colors A, B and C for crochet trim
One pair No.6 needles
(or Canadian No.7)
One No.E (3.50 mm)
crochet hook

Wagon wheel scarf
Sports Yarn
2 balls main color A, white
1 ball each of contrast colors

Wagon wheel scarf
B, orange, C, gold, D, tangerine, E, medium brown and F, dark brown
One No.G (4.50 mm)
crochet hook

Crazy stitch scarf
Sports Yarn
3 balls
One No.G (4.50 mm)
crochet hook

Plaid scarf
Sports Yarn
3 balls main color A, brown
2 balls contrast color B, red and 2 balls contrast color C, white
One No.F (4.00 mm)
crochet hook

Basket stitch scarf
Sports Yarn
4 balls
One pair No.7 needles
(or Canadian No.6)

Chevron striped scarf

Using No.5 needles and A, cast on 56 sts. Work in chevron stripe (see Knitting Know-how chapter 23, page 442), working 36 rows A, 12 rows B, 2 rows A and 12 rows B 9 times in all, ending with 35 rows A.
K1 row.
Bind off.
Seam long edges tog on WS. Turn to RS. Work small spirals in both colors (see Crochet Know-how chapter 8, page 146 crochet know-how) and sew to points.

Lace fringed scarf

Using No.5 needles, cast on 45 sts. Work in ivy leaf stitch (see Knitting Know-how chapter 29, page 562). Continue until work measures 76in or desired length.
Bind off.
Work fringe on both short

▲ Left to right; scarf in chevron stripes; in lace stitch with a fringe;

ends (see Knitting Know-how chapter 4, page 62).

Woven stitch scarf

Using No.6 needles, cast on 3 sts. Work in woven vertical stitch (see Knitting Know-how chapter 24, page 462) until work measures 84in or desired length. Bind off. Trim with 6 rows crochet edging (see Crochet Know-how chapter 19, page 364) or star motif (see Crochet Know-how chapter 12, page 226).

woven stitch scarf; the wagon wheel pattern; a scarf in crazy stitch; a plaid scarf; and one in basket stitch

Wagon wheel scarf

Use No. G crochet hook. Work large circles from the wagon wheel design (see Crochet Know-how chapter 11, page 206), working from beg to end of 3rd round only. This scarf uses 3 colors for each circle in 4 different combinations of colors. Work 13 wheels using A, B and C and 13 using A, E and F. Work 14 using A, C and B and 14 using A, D and F. Small circles are worked in A and use the first round only. Work 26 small circles. Sew the edges of large circles tog, sewing a small circle in center space between 4 circles.

Crazy stitch scarf

Using No. G crochet hook, ch32. Continue in crazy stitch (see Crochet Know-how chapter 25, page 486) for 84 in. or desired length. Fasten off. Trim with deep fringe (see Kntting Know-how chapter 4, page 62).

Plaid scarf

Using No. F crochet hook and A, ch39. Continue working mesh background (see Crochet Know-how chapter 36, page 706), working 12 rows A, 1 row C, 3 rows B, 1 row C alt, ending with 12 rows A. When work measures 84 in. or desired length, fasten off. Using yarn double, work vertical stripes in following sequence, working from right to left (1 row C, 2B, 1C, 3A) twice, ending with 1 row C, 2B, 1C.

Basket stitch scarf

Using No. 7 needles, cast on 40 sts. Work in basket stitch (see Knitting Know-how chapter 5, page 82) for 96 in. or desired length. Bind off. Trim with large pompon at either end (see Crochet Know-how chapter 14, page 266).

1085

Technique of Tunisian crochet

To be able to make garments in Tunisian crochet it is necessary to understand how to increase and decrease while working the fabric. This chapter also explains how to make buttonholes in this afghan stitch.

The method of working Tunisian crochet makes it easy to work with two yarns simultaneously, a technique which can be used with many of the stitches to achieve tweed-like textures and a thickness of fabric which is not always possible with ordinary crochet. Experiment with two different weights of yarn for a tweedy look.

Increasing one stitch at beginning of a row

To increase one stitch at the beginning of a right side row, or the right-hand edge of the work, work 1 chain then insert the hook under the horizontal thread between the first and second upright threads, yrh and draw through one loop. Continue working into next and following upright threads in the normal way.

Increasing one stitch at end of a row

Work in the same way as given for the beginning of the row by inserting the hook under the horizontal thread between the second to last and last stitches, yrh and draw through one loop. Work the last stitch in the usual way.

Increasing two or more stitches at beginning of a row

To increase more than one stitch at the beginning of a row, work that number of chains. Into the chain work classic Tunisian stitch and continue along the row.

Increasing two or more stitches at end of a row

At the left-hand end of a right side row, put onto the hook the required number of slip stitches. Continue to work the next row in the usual way.

Decreasing one stitch at right-hand edge

Insert the hook through 2 upright threads, yrh and draw through only one loop, working to the end of the row in the normal way.

Decreasing one stitch at end of a row

Work in the same way as given for the beginning of a row by inserting the hook through the last 2 upright threads together, yrh and draw through only one loop.

Working a buttonhole

Mark the position for a buttonhole with pins on the right side of the work before beginning the right side row. Work to the beginning of the marked position. Wind yarn around the hook for the number of stitches over which the hole must stretch, skip this number of stitches and continue to the end of the row. On the next row, work off each loop of yarn as if it were one stitch.

▲ *Increasing one stitch at the beginning of a row*

▲ *Increasing one stitch at the end of a row*
▼ *Increasing two or more stitches at the beginning of a row*

▼ *Increasing two or more stitches at the end of a row*

▲ *Decreasing one stitch at the right-hand edge*

▲ *Winding yarn around the hook for a buttonhole*
▼ *Working the 2nd row of the buttonhole*

Tunisian rib stitch

Worked over an even number of chains.

1st and 2nd rows. As given for classic Tunisian stitch (see Crochet Know-how 54, page 1066).

3rd row. Ch1, *insert hook into 3rd upright thread of previous row, yrh and draw through one loop, insert hook into 2nd upright thread, yrh and draw through one loop, continue from * in this way working in groups of 2 and crossing the threads by working the 5th then 4th, 7th then 6th, etc, ending with one st in last upright thread.

4th row. As classic Tunisian stitch.

Repeat 3rd and 4th rows as desired. If this pattern is worked over stitches which are being decreased or increased, be careful to see that the crossed stitches come immediately above the crossed stitches of the previous row, or the ribbed effect will be slightly irregular.

Tunisian diagonal rib stitch

Worked over an even number of chains.

1st and 2nd rows. Work as given for classic Tunisian stitch.

3rd and 4th rows. Work as given for rib stitch.

5th row. Ch1, work into next upright thread, yrh and draw loop through, then work one stitch into each of next 2 stitches, working the furthest away first then returning to work the skipped one, rep to end of row.

6th row. As given for 2nd row of classic Tunisian stitch.

Repeat 3rd to 6th rows as required.

Tunisian cluster stitch

This stitch can be varied to obtain different patterns.

It is worked on a ground of classic Tunisian stitch, working the clusters where required by chaining 4 or 5 before working the next stitch. The chain or cluster formed should be left on the right side of the work. Use cluster stitch spaced evenly on the surface as an all-over pattern, or grouped together in geometric designs.

▲ *Tunisian rib stitch*

▲ *Tunisian diagonal rib stitch*
▼ *Tunisian cluster stitch*

Cushioned with an apple

This succulent apple motif for a pillow in vibrant colors shows an interesting use of chain stitch for a bold effect.

To make the pillow 16 inches by 16 inches you will need:

□ ½yd 36 inch wide even-weave linen
□ Pillow form 1 inch larger than finished size of pillow
□ Mercerized sewing thread to match background fabric
□ D.M.C. Six-strand floss in the following colors: One skein orange 608; one

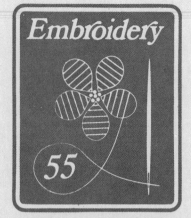

skein dark green 700; two skeins green 3346
□ D.M.C. Matte Embroidery cotton in the following colors: Four skeins red 2349; two skeins pink 2776
□ 12 inch zipper
□ Tracing paper
□ Graph paper

To enlarge the design

Trace and enlarge the design to measure 11 inches from the tip of the top leaf to the lower edge of the apple. Trace the enlarged design onto tracing paper.

Transferring the design

Fold the fabric and cut the piece in two. Mark the center with rows of basting stitches each way. Work a line of basting stitches 2 inches in from the outer edges to form a square measuring 16 inches by 16 inches, to mark the outer edges of the pillow. Pin the traced design in position $2\frac{3}{4}$ inches up from the lower line of basting stitches and centering the design between the two vertical lines. Using the matching sewing thread transfer the design to the background fabric, stitching all the lines of design through the tracing paper. When all the lines have been marked with basting the paper is torn away. If the basting stitches are well covered with embroidery they need not be removed when the design is completed.

Stitches

Begin with the orange shape. Use six strands of floss, and start the chain stitching from the outer edge of each shape, working toward the center. This insures a well defined outline. Work the deep pink area next and finally the red. Leave gaps in the chain stitch filling where indicated on the design and fill these with bullion knots. The bullion knots are also worked with six strands of floss and with three twists around the needle. Work the apple leaves in outline stitch filling with the veins in outline stitch, using four strands of floss. The calyx at the bottom of the apple is formed by working three detached chain stitches one inside the other starting with the outer. The stem is worked in four separate rows of outline stitch using four strands of floss.

To make the pillow

When the embroidery is completed, press the work lightly over a damp cloth and a thick, soft pad to avoid flattening the bullion knots.
Make the cushion according to the instructions given in Embroidery chapter 18, page 348, and insert the pillow form.

▼ *Trace and enlarge this design to the required size*

1089

Collector's Piece

Flowers in fabric

The designer of these appliqué and embroidery pictures has used the colors, textures and surface patterns of fabrics as a graphic artist uses pigments and brush strokes to achieve an effect. The poppy picture, for instance, uses for the background a gold colored stripe weaved curtain fabric which produces an effect of wheat stalks in sunshine. In each of the designs, the petal edges and the leaf edges have been left free of the background fabric to give a more life-like impression, and this technique is very noticeable in the poppy design. The Christmas roses are worked on a background of Moygashel dress fabric with the flower petals made of white satin, white velvet and pink grosgrain. The petals are applied to the background with long basting stitches, reproducing the natural crumpled look of the rose petals themselves. The rose centers are padded and decorated with seed pearls and French knots worked in plastic raffia and silk.

▼ *Christmas roses using satin, velvet and grosgrain for the petals*   *Brilliant poppy heads against an effect of sunlit wheat stalks* ▶

A very dignified teddy bear

Theodore Bear, an animal of some dignity, is simple to make from fur fabric and felt. A graph for the pattern pieces is given on the opposite page with full instructions to help you make this worthy addition to your household.

Suitable fabrics
Nylon fur or any synthetic fur fabric is suitable for a teddy bear, as these fabrics are spongeable. Check that the dye in the fabric is fast, since most children are rather fervent in the love that they lavish on their toys, even to the extent of chewing them!

You will need
- ☐ ½yd fur fabric 54in wide, for the body
- ☐ Two 9in squares brown felt for the feet and ears
- ☐ A scrap of black felt for the nose
- ☐ 3ft black sports yarn for embroidering the features

▼ *Theodore, a teddy bear of great dignity and charm*

- ☐ Four 1½in wooden disk joints
- ☐ Pair of Safety Eyes and fixing tool
- ☐ 1lb bag Kapok or Dacron fiber filling for stuffing
- ☐ Matching sewing thread, basting thread, strong linen thread
- ☐ 1yd 1½in wide satin ribbon
- ☐ Pliers
- ☐ A pair of very sharp scissors
- ☐ Darning needle

Making the pattern
You will need:
- ☐ Large sheet, 20in x 20in, of 1½inch squared paper. Either rule brown paper or use graph paper
- ☐ Pencil
- ☐ Paper cutting scissors

Copy all the pattern shapes and their markings from the graph onto the squared paper, one square on the graph being equal to a 1½ inch square on the paper.
Cut out the pattern pieces.

Cutting out
Each pattern piece gives complete cutting instructions which include the name and number of the pattern piece, how many to cut, what seam allowance will be needed and the direction of the fabric pile.
Pin pattern pieces 1,2,3,4,5, 8,9 and 10 onto the right side of the single fur fabric with the pile of the fur running in the direction indicated by the arrows on the pattern pieces.
Cut out around the pattern pieces with the tips of the sharp scissors to avoid spoiling the pile, adding seam allowances where indicated.
Pin pattern pieces 6, 7, 8 and 11 to the felt and cut out, adding seam allowances where indicated.
On all the fabric pieces mark the positions of letters A to Y where indicated, using basting thread.

Making the teddy bear
Machine stitch around the edges of all the fur fabric pieces and then overcast all the raw edges. This will strengthen the fur fabric and will prevent fraying.

The body
Place the two front body pieces together, fur sides facing, and stitch them from C to F. Place the back body piece to the joined fronts, fur sides facing, and stitch from E to F to E. Turn the body fur side out.

The arms and legs
Make the arms by first stitching each paw to each forearm, felt to fur side, from P to Q. Then stitch each forearm and paw to each arm, fur sides facing, around the edges, leaving an opening where shown on the pattern.
Turn fur side out.
Make the legs in pairs, fur sides facing, by stitching from M to X and N to Y. Sew in the felt foot pads by hand using back stitch, matching points X and Y. Turn fur side out.
Stuff each of the arms and legs firmly leaving room at the top to insert the joints.

Jointing
Each joint consists of two wooden disks and a cotter pin.
From the remaining felt cut eight circles each slightly larger than the wooden disks. Take one wooden disk off each cotter pin and replace it with a felt circle.
On one of the legs push a cotter pin through the fabric from the inside to the outside, where it is marked with a star, so that the felt circle and wooden disk are inside the leg. Then pack stuffing tightly around the disk and finish stuffing the leg. Close the opening with a slip stitch.
Repeat this with the other leg and the two arms.
To join the limbs to the body, again take one of the legs and push the cotter pin through the body of the bear from the outside to the inside where marked. Place a second felt circle onto the cotter pin and then put the original wooden disk back onto the cotter pin so that the second felt circle and wooden disk are inside the body of the bear. Take the pliers and bend the cotter pin open so that the joint is as tight as possible.

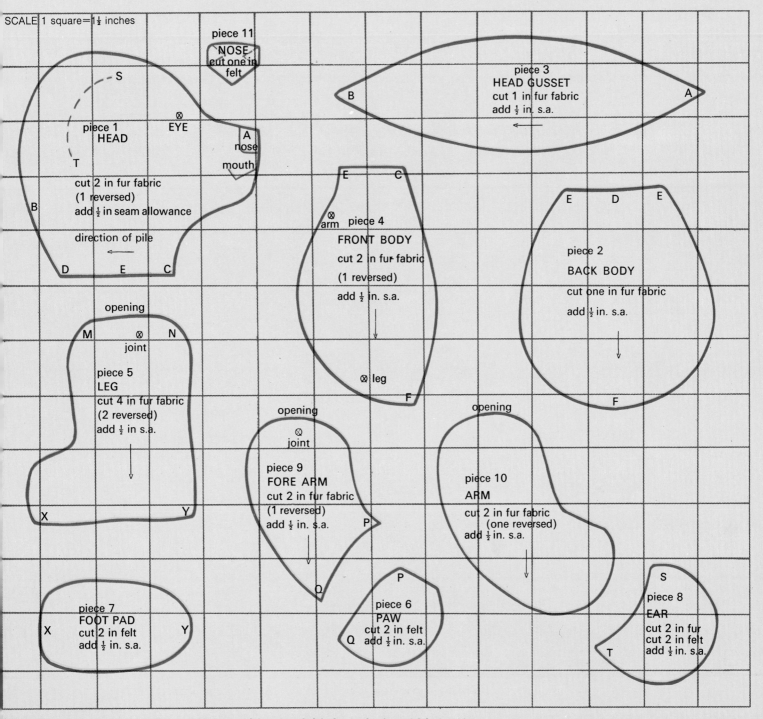

SCALE 1 square=1½ inches

piece 11
NOSE
cut one in felt

S

piece 1
HEAD
EYE
A
nose
mouth
T
B
cut 2 in fur fabric
(1 reversed)
add ½ in seam allowance

direction of pile

D   E   C

piece 3
HEAD GUSSET
cut 1 in fur fabric
add ½ in. s.a.
B   A

E   C
⊗ arm   piece 4
FRONT BODY
cut 2 in fur fabric
(1 reversed)
add ½ in. s.a.

⊗ leg
F

E   D   E

piece 2
BACK BODY
cut one in fur fabric
add ½ in. s.a.

F

opening
M   ⊗   N
joint

piece 5
LEG
cut 4 in fur fabric
(2 reversed)
add ½ in s.a.

X   Y

opening
⊗ joint

piece 9
FORE ARM
cut 2 in fur fabric
(1 reversed)
add ½ in. s.a.
P

Q

opening

piece 10
ARM
cut 2 in fur fabric
(one reversed)
add ½ in. s.a.

S

piece 8
EAR
cut 2 in fur
cut 2 in felt
add ½ in. s.a.
T

piece 7
FOOT PAD
cut 2 in felt
add ½ in. s.a.
X   Y

P

piece 6
PAW
cut 2 in felt
Q   add ½ in. s.a.

▲ *Graph for the pattern pieces of the teddy bear which, when finished, stands about 16 inches high*

Join the other leg and arms to the body in the same way.

Stuffing the body
Stuff the body through the neck opening and then, using a strong linen thread, make a row of gathering stitches around the neck opening ½in from the edge. Pull the gathering stitches tight.

The head
Attach one Safety Eye to each head piece where indicated,

using the fixing tool.
Stitch the head gusset to the head pieces by stitching one head piece to one side of the head gusset, fur sides facing, matching A to B and then stitching the other head piece to the other side of the head gusset in the same way. Then join head seams B to D and A to C, fur sides facing.
Turn the head fur side out and stuff it firmly.
Take the felt nose piece and make darts where indicated by

the dotted lines. Put a little stuffing into the nose and sew it into place at A.
Embroider the mouth with sports yarn.
Make the ears using one felt piece and one fur fabric piece for each ear. Stitch each pair together around the outer curved side, then turn the ears right side out and sew them to the head, matching S to T.

Joining the head to the body
Using the strong linen thread,

run a row of gathering stitches around the neck ½in from the edge and pull tight.
Turn the seam allowance on the neck edge of the body inside, push the seam allowance of the head inside the body so that the stitching lines correspond. Firmly overcast the head to the body using the linen thread. Hide these stitches by tying the satin ribbon around the teddy bear's neck.
Embroider the claws with the sports yarn.

Lace from the sun

Teneriffe lace, one of the famous "sun" laces popular in 16th century Spain, is worked separately while other sun laces are worked on cloth. Here is the basic technique and several ideas for decorating motifs.

Teneriffe lace takes its name from the largest of the Canary Islands, where it is made and sold to tourists. It can be worked in many shapes—squares, ovals, diamonds and straight borders, but the pattern most widely used is the circular star. Each star is made separately and then sewn to the material or joined to other stars.

Materials you will need
- [ ] Compass
- [ ] Thin cardboard
- [ ] Tracing paper or transparent fabric
- [ ] Pencil
- [ ] Ruler
- [ ] Long needle with blunt end (J. & P. Coat's tapestry needle)
- [ ] Strong thread for support stitches (J. & P. Coat's Super Sheen No.40)
- [ ] Thread (Clark's Big Ball Mercerized Crochet Cotton Size 40, Coats & Clark's O.N.T. Pearl Cotton)

Making the pattern
Although the illustrations only show support stitches, it is simplest for a beginner to draw out the pattern in lines on thin cardboard forming the star shaped base on which the designs are worked.

Using a compass, draw a circle between $2\frac{1}{2}$ to $3\frac{1}{2}$ inches in diameter. With a ruler, divide the circle in half, then quarters, and so on until you have up to 32 equally spaced segments. Again, as a rule this is the simplest number for a beginner to work with although the number can vary. There is, in fact, an odd number of segments in the illustrations in this chapter.

Draw several concentric circles within the outline circle for the positioning of the decorative stitches.

Place the tracing paper or fabric over the cardboard and secure with basting stitches forming an outside square.

Working the support stitches
Using the strong thread, make running stitch between the spokes, going across the edge of every alternate segment, then go around a second time to fill in the alternate segment previously missed.

Working the star
Make the spokes by starting at the center of the circle with a knot on the wrong side. This can be cut off afterward, once the last spoke has been worked and knotted to the first one. Take the yarn up through one support stitch, down through the one to the left of this, and straight across to the support stitch exactly opposite, down through this and up through the stitch to the right.

1094

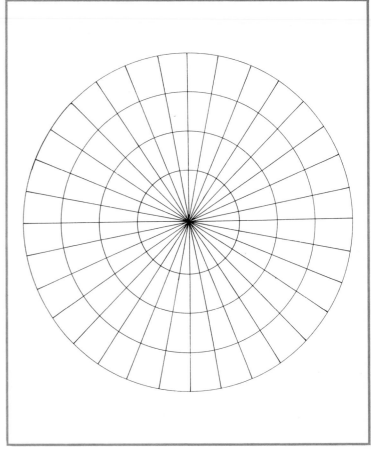

▲ *The basic pattern outline of a Teneriffe motif with thirty-two spokes*

To make the next spoke take the thread up and through the left-hand support stitch which has already been used, down through the support stitch to the left, across to the right-hand stitch which has already been used and back up through the stitch to the right of this.

Continue until all the spokes have been worked. Finish off by taking the thread to the center and knot it neatly to the beginning. Do not cut the thread.

Secure the center of the star at the crossing point with the same thread, working darning stitch over and under the spokes. Each time you complete a round and have returned to the point where you started weaving, take up two stitches together to maintain the alternated woven effect with the previous row. Work as many rows as the desired effect requires, being careful not to pull the thread too tightly or you will draw in the star, distorting the shape. As Teneriffe work is seen from both sides, any joins in the yarn must be as small as possible, and the neatest method is to use a weaver's knot.

An alternative method is to work only one row of running stitches for the support stitches so that the top of the spokes have a much more open effect.

Decorating the star
The spokes are finally held in place by working concentric circles of knotting and interlacing and these in turn can be decorated with contrast interlacings. A few examples are illustrated from which you will be able to develop ideas of your own.

Finishing off
Once the star is completed, cut the support stitches to free the star from the cardboard and either join it to subsequent stars or mount it to or insert it in fabric.

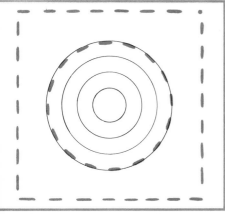

Working the first round of running stitches

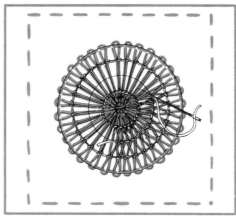

▲ *Rounds of knotting and interlacing*

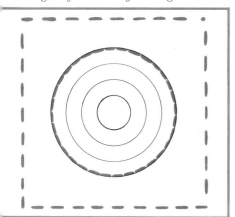

The second round of stitches fills the spaces

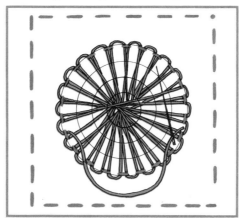

▲ *Openwork spokes using every second stitch*

▲ *Open Cretan stitch between rows of knotting*

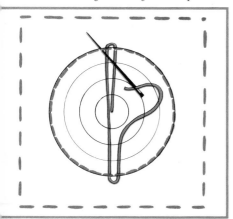

Laying the first spokes of the star
Example of Teneriffe motif with open spokes ▶
The star halfway to completion of the spokes

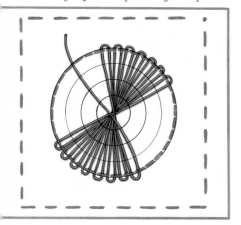

Making a fitted slip

Nothing is nicer for a party than a dress made in a floaty, sheer fabric. Often these dresses are unlined and then the problem arises of what to wear underneath. The obvious answer is a simple, well fitting slip that molds to your body. Sometimes, even a well fitting slip in a neutral color can be hard to come by, so if you have a dress which really needs well shaped undergarments and where an attached lining would add too much bulk in the seams, a fitted slip pattern provides an ideal and easy answer. Another good reason for substituting a fitted slip for a lining is that some dress fabrics require special treatment for cleaning which could ruin the fabric of an attached lining.

The slip featured in this chapter is a version of the basic dress pattern from the Creative Hands Pattern Pack. It has body darts and attractive contour darting added to the Center Front so that it fits properly over the bustline giving a smooth finish.

Full instructions are given here for making the basic slip, but there is no reason why you should not make it longer or shorter, shaped at the top or trimmed in any way you wish. In addition, if you already have a commercial paper pattern for a simple dress style, you can use the same methods for converting it to a slip.

Choosing the right fabric

You should use the same care when choosing fabric for a slip as you would for dress linings. In the following paragraphs suitable and unsuitable fabrics are featured to help you avoid making mistakes.

Suitable fabrics

The suitable fabrics are the ones which have some weight and firmness. For these choose from the wide range of washable lingerie taffetas made in nylon, rayon and other synthetics.

You may choose a stiff quality if the outer garment is made in a heavy fabric, but for more versatile use choose one of the softer taffetas in the above mentioned fibers. These will tailor better and mold to the body and can therefore be worn under a variety of dress fabrics without making impressions on the outside, and yet they are strong enough for hard wear.

Other suitable fabrics are the traditional, old fashioned lingerie crêpes made from pure or artificial silks, but these can be difficult to find.

Nylon and Dacron satins are ideal, and a cheap but good quality satin de Lys and crêpe de Lys is available which is a mixture of nylon, polyester and silk fibers.

Nylon and other synthetic jerseys, which are not too fine and have a feeling of some weight, can be used very successfully, especially if you have an automatic or zigzag sewing machine.

If you are making a slip to wear under a see-through voile dress, choose a plain lightweight dress fabric.

Unsuitable fabrics

The most unsuitable fabrics are those which hold static electricity. Not only does this distort the fit of the slip, but it also interferes with the hang of the garment worn over it.

These fabrics are mostly in the finer weaves and are usually man-made, although some silks will also cling. Here is a reliable test to see if the fabric is suitable.

Static electricity test. Lay a length of fabric on the store counter and stroke it with your hand several times. Most fabrics will develop some electricity with this treatment, but avoid the ones which do not lie flat and which form air pockets and folds as you try to straighten them out. These are the fabrics which can not be made successfully into a slip as they will always cling.

Suitable for sheers

You must also test for static electricity when you are making a slip to go under sheer fabrics, especially chiffon. Some taffetas will make chiffon cling to them although the taffeta itself shows no sign of static electricity. Be sure to test the combination of the fabrics before you start.

Longer slips

You may find that in spite of all your precautions static electricity occurs with longer slips because of the area involved. To give the garment a little more weight to counteract this, insert a fine roll of covered lead pellet weights into the fold of the hemline. Lead pellets are easily obtainable in the curtain or notion departments of stores.

Finding the correct finish

A fitted slip must fit smoothly and must not have bulky seams which would cause impressions on the outside of a garment. But although the finish must be kept as flat as possible, it must be strong enough to withstand really hard wear. In addition, this type of garment fits close to the body and is subject to body moisture, which weakens the structure of the fabric and the seams.

In the old tradition lingerie was finished by hand, but it is best to finish modern fabrics by machine. French seaming may be used in soft fabrics, but the seams in the stronger or heavier fabrics must be kept flat like dress seams and finished inside in the same way.

The upper edge of the slip can be finished in many ways. The one featured in this chapter lends itself to a plain or trimmed finish. For hem finishes other than the one used here, turn to Dress-making chapter 21, page 416, where you will find a number of suitable alternatives are shown.

The slip pattern

Copy the Front and Back dress pattern pieces (numbers 1 and 2) from the Pattern Pack.

Before cutting out the pattern pieces, add 1 inch to the side seam of the Front between the armhole and the darts as shown (figure 1). Next, reduce the ease on both the Front and Back as the slip has to fit closer to the body than the dress. To do this, deduct $\frac{1}{8}$ inch from the Center Front and Center Back and $\frac{1}{4}$ inch from each side seam, including the bit added to the side Front.

Cut out both pattern pieces.

Bust darts

For a perfect fit it is very important that all horizontal darts

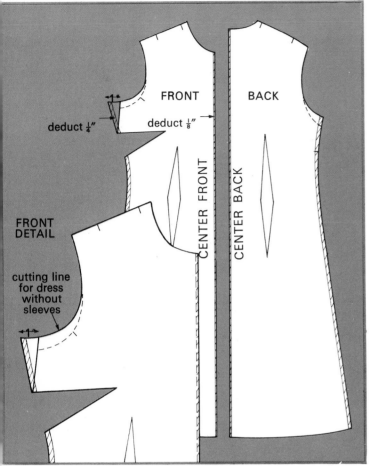

FRONT

BACK

deduct ¼"

deduct ⅛"

FRONT DETAIL

cutting line for dress without sleeves

CENTER FRONT

CENTER BACK

▲ **1.** *Adding to the Front side seam and reducing the ease on Front and Back*
The fitted slip is adaptable to any dress length, style or color ►

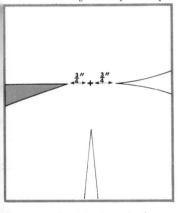

¾" ¾"

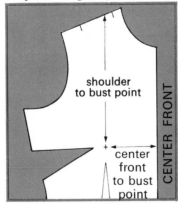

shoulder to bust point

center front to bust point

CENTER FRONT

▲ **2.** *Detail of the front darting*   ▲ **3.** *Marking the bust point*

(see figure **2**) run toward the point of the bust but never actually onto the point as this would create a ridge. So all darts should end ¾ inch from the bust point.

Marking the bust point. You can use the bodice muslin to find the correct position of the bust point, if you have made one, otherwise just measure on your body.

Measure the distance from bust point to bust point. Then, starting on the Center Front line, mark off half this measurement on the Front pattern.

Measure the depth from shoulder to bust point and mark the pattern where both points coincide (figure **3**).

Using a 45° triangle on the Center Front, draw a line straight across the pattern through the bust mark. If your basic dress pattern was adjusted accurately on a previous occasion this line should touch the pointed end of the dart.

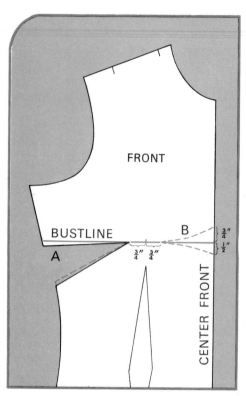

▲ 4. *Marking out the horizontal darts A and B*

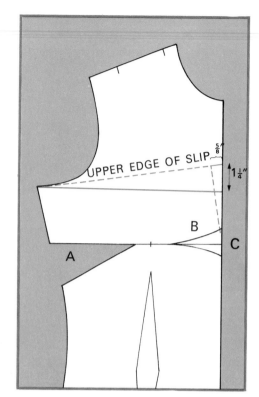

▲ 5. *Marking the upper edge and vertical dart*

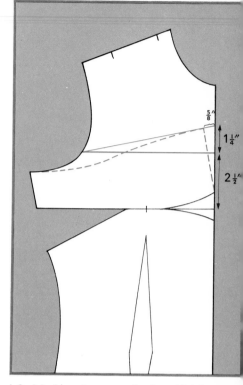

▲ 6. *Marking the upper edge for a high bust*

The side bust dart (A). Raise the slant of the side bust dart, using the bustline for the upper stitching line. Raise the lower stitching line by the same amount (figure **4**).

If necessary, adjust the dart point $\frac{3}{4}$ inches from the bust point marking.

The Center Front horizontal dart (B). Mark the dart point $\frac{3}{4}$ inches from the bust mark toward the Center Front (figure **4**).

The depth of the dart is $1\frac{1}{4}$ inches. Mark $\frac{1}{2}$ inch below the bustline and $\frac{3}{4}$ inch above on the Center Front. Draw in the dart, curving it as shown.

Finding the upper edge of the slip. Except in the case of a very high bustline, draw a straight line across the Front pattern from underarm to Center Front, parallel to the bustline.

To keep the upper edge of the slip looking straight, you must compensate for the depth of the horizontal dart by raising it $1\frac{1}{4}$ inches at the Center Front and tapering to nothing as shown (figure **5**).

If you have a very high bustline, work exactly as above but draw the upper line $2\frac{1}{2}$ inches above the bustline and curve it out of the underarm line (figure **6**).

Vertical dart (C). To fit the cleavage, make a dart as shown (figure **5**), measuring $\frac{5}{8}$ inch in from the Center Front along the upper edge, tapering to nothing on dart B.

Finishing the pattern

Mark the upper edge on the Back in line with the upper edge on the Front in the

side seam and curve it slightly down at the Center Back as shown (figure **7**).

Mark a 14 inch opening in the side seams on both Front and Back pattern pieces, starting at the upper edge of the slip. Adjust the pattern length as required, then cut out along the new lines.

A final word

As the slip has to be so closely and carefully fitted to the body, the depth and positions of the darts serve only as a guide at this stage—they may well have to be adjusted later.

If you should suspect that you may have to deepen the darts, it is wise to add a little more than the usual seam allowance.

Yardages, notions, cutting out

Layout and fabric requirements

Make a layout as shown in Dressmaking Chapter 46, page 916, placing the Center Back and Center Front on the fold of the fabric. Add seam allowances and 2 inches for the hem. Also include an extra $\frac{3}{8}$ yard in the yardage to be used for a bias facing to finish the top edge.

Notions

You will also need
- [ ] 14 inch fine nylon zipper
- [ ] Matching satin or taffeta ribbon for shoulder straps
- [ ] Small hook
- [ ] Matching thread

Cutting

Using the layout, cut out the fabric.

Carefully mark the pattern details on the fabric including the shape of the side seams. This is necessary so that you can check the adjustments to each side at the fitting stage.

Fitting

Pin and baste the darts and the side seams, leaving an opening in the left side for the zipper.

Use tape or ribbon to stand in for the shoulder straps at the fitting. Pin them to the basted garment, so that they are in line with the darts in the Back and $\frac{3}{4}$ inch to the outside of the center of the bust in Front. Leave some extra length on the tape or ribbon to make adjustments.

The first fitting

Fitting the slip is done in two stages. The first stage should always be done with the garment inside out, except if you know you have uneven sides. Then it is safer to fit the slip with the right side out. (For the first fitting for uneven sides see the following instructions.)

Put on the slip and pin the opening together in the side seams. This is now on the right side of your body.

Check that the bustline of the slip is perfectly in line with your own and that all the dart points run toward it; if not, raise or lower it with shoulder straps. Start fitting the bustline first and take out

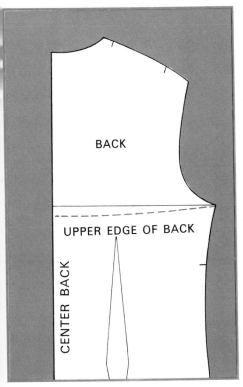

▲ **7.** *Marking the upper edge on the Back*

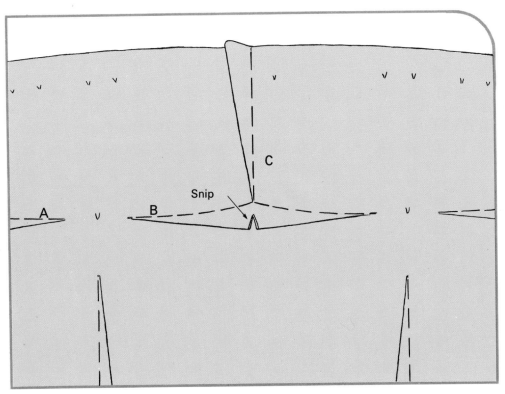

▲ **8.** *Snipping the horizontal dart for the second fitting*

any fullness by pinning it into the side seams at this point.

Next fit the Center Front darts so that they curve into the bust contour and run out flat onto the bust.

If you have a very large bust, you may need to take the horizontal darting in more deeply. It then becomes necessary to make a second horizontal dart $\frac{1}{2}$ inch below the original one to stop the dragging from under the bustline which would occur if all the fullness was lifted into one dart. Do not deepen the original dart, but try and take all the extra depth into the second dart, which is parallel to the first but will be slightly shorter because it does not run toward the bust point.

If you make any alterations to the horizontal dart, you will find that the vertical dart also needs adjusting.

Taking in the vertical dart may result in tightness at the upper edge, and you will have to compensate for this by letting out from the side seams.

Adjust the side bust darts if necessary.

Any surplus fabric around the midriff and the waistline should first be pinned off into the Front and Back body darts. Here too, the fitting will vary with each figure shape and the fullness may have to be distributed between the darts and the side seams. If you find, when making the body darts deeper, that drag lines show toward the side seams, stop and pin the rest into the side seams.

The shoulder straps should now feel comfortable and not drag the garment.

First fitting for uneven sides

If you have the problem of uneven sides, especially differences in the bust height, it is necessary to fit the slip right side out. You will have to pin and baste the Center Front horizontal dart on the outside of the garment because the depth of the dart on the inside would make the line stretch across the front and prevent your checking if it is correct. The dart is turned to the inside of the garment after the fitting. Fit the rest of the slip, using the same sequence as above.

The second fitting

Correct all the fitting faults and prepare the garment for a second basted fitting. Snip carefully into the depth of the horizontal dart in the Center Front halfway as shown (figure **8**). This way you will be able to check if the ends of the dart run out smoothly.

Baste in the zipper fastener. Put on the slip right side out, and stand before a mirror with your arms beside your body.

At this stage the slip should fit closely, but not tightly, over the bust and the waistline. All the darts should run out flat toward the bust and not create any folds or creases.

If there is lift in the ends of the darts, it means that you have slightly overfitted them and you will have to let them out a little.

Do not try to pin off any fullness at the dart points; this only makes the problem worse and you would have to make one

dart end run into the other to get rid of this fullness.

Move around, stoop and bend and then sit down. It must be a close fit, but it must not strain in the seams.

Check the strap positions. If the slip is to be worn under sheer garments, they should be directly in line with the straps of your bra.

Make sure at this stage that the upper edge of the slip has remained straight. Pin the seam allowance under along the front edge and see where adjustments are necessary. Finally, try a dress over the slip to make sure that you have the correct length adjustments, and your slip will be ready for stitching.

Making the slip

Before removing the tailor's tacking and the basting stitches, transfer all the fitting corrections of the slip to your paper pattern. This will allow you to work more quickly when you want to make up the pattern again.

The darts

First stitch the horizontal dart (B). Trim the inside fold to $\frac{1}{8}$ inch and snip it at the Center Front to within a few grains of the stitching line (figure **9**). Carefully finish the raw edges together, taking special care with the snipped edge, and press the dart downward.

Next, stitch the vertical dart (C). Slash it along the center to within $\frac{3}{4}$ inch of the end, trim the seam allowance to $\frac{3}{8}$ inch

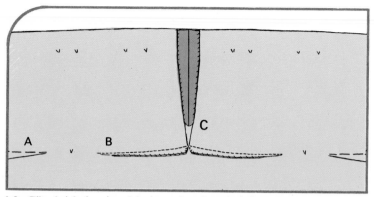

▲ **9.** *The finished, snipped horizontal and vertical darts*

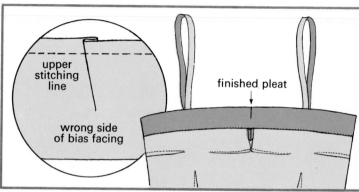

▲ **11.** *The inverted miter on the bias facing at the Center Front*

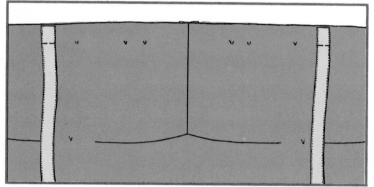

▲ **10.** *Basting the straps to the upper edge of the slip on the right side*

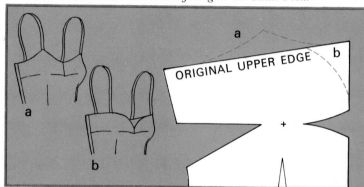

▲ **12.** *Alternative shapes for the upper edge of the slip*

and press the dart open (figure **9**). Finish the raw edges.

To stitch the side bust darts (A), rip the right side seam sufficiently to enable you to work on the dart.

Stitch the darts and trim the depth of the dart fold to ⅜ inch, finish the raw edges together and press the darts down.

Stitch the body darts on the Front and Back and press them toward the center. To relieve any strain in the dart fold, make a small snip.

Side seams

Stitch the side seams, using the method suitable for the type of fabric.

For French seams, prepare the zipper opening as follows:

Start 1 inch below the balance mark for the end of the opening and, with wrong sides together, stitch the seam as for the first row of stitches for a French seam.

Trim the seam allowance along the stitched section only from 1 inch below the balance mark to the hem. Turn the seam to the inside in the usual way and make the second row of stitches, starting at the balance mark, to cover the raw edges of the first row of stitches.

Fasten off the ends of the thread carefully at the balance mark.

Next, pin and baste the seam allowance on the opening to the inside of the garment and insert the zipper in the normal way. If you find that the seam allowance strains where it folds into the French

seam, rip the first row of stitches a fraction until the seam allowance rolls into the French seam without strain.

Press the French seams toward the front and finish the raw edges of the seam allowance on the opening. Do not be tempted to snip the seam allowance, since this would weaken the seam here.

The shoulder straps

For the shoulder straps, use a matching satin ribbon, which is nice and strong, or taffeta ribbon. You can also make a narrow tube of self fabric ½ inch wide, which is cut on the straight of the grain. Pin and baste the seam allowance of the right side of the straps to the seam allowance of the right side of the upper edge of the garment, raw edges even, so that the seam allowance of the straps can be caught in with the bias facing (figure **10**).

The facing

To make a bias facing, cut a strip of bias fabric from the rest of the fabric 1¼ inches wide, long enough to fit the length of the upper edge of the slip. If you must join the bias strip, make the seams so that they correspond with the garment.

To avoid straining the lower edge of the strip when it is turned to the inside of the garment at the Center Front, add ½ inch to the length measurement and make an inverted miter in line with the seamline of the vertical dart. To do this, make a small pleat in the bias along the

upper stitching line as shown (figure **11**). This means you can then stitch the lower edge of the facing to the slip without it straining over the dart seam. Stitch on the bias facing as given in Dressmaking chapter 11, page 216, but do not curve it. Sew on a hook and hand-work a bar at the top of the side opening.

The hem

The hem finishes featured in Dressmaking chapter 21, page 416, are suitable for the fitted slip. Do not hand sew the hem in place. The constant friction of nylon stockings on the hem when walking will actually fray the sewing thread and the hem will need constant repair.

Make firm small machine stitches along the folded edge of the hem allowance—they will be more durable.

Alternative shapes for the upper edge

When fitting the slip it is easy to alter the shape of the upper straight edge into a center front dip, or raise it to follow the line of your bra (figure **12**).

This can be done without fear that the basic fitting structure will be affected. Face the shaped edge with a bias facing which must be carefully mitered in dips and points so that it corresponds with the top of the garment. It is best to fit the strip and pin the miters as necessary as you work. Take off the bias strip and then stitch the miters by machine and press the seams open. This will give you a good flat finish.